BUMBLING WITH THE ARABS
ALL THE WAY TO THE BANK

BUMBLING WITH THE ARABS

All the Way to the Bank

BEN KOSHKIN

Bumbling With the Arabs All the Way to the Bank

© 2023 by Ben Koshkin

Editors: River Chau, Regina Cornell, Deborah Froese
Cover Design: Rachel Hogue
Interior Design: Emma Elzinga

Indigo River Publishing
3 West Garden Street, Ste. 718
Pensacola, FL 32502
www.indigoriverpublishing.com

Ordering Information:
Quantity sales: Special discounts are available on quantity purchases by corporations, associations, and others. For details, contact the publisher at the address above.
Orders by US trade bookstores and wholesalers: Please contact the publisher at the address above.

Printed in the United States of America

Library of Congress Control Number: 2019951185
ISBN: 978-1-950906-19-2 (paperback), 978-1-950906-24-6 (ebook)

First Edition

With Indigo River Publishing, you can always expect great books, strong voices, and meaningful messages. Most importantly, you'll always find . . . *words worth reading.*

TABLE OF CONTENTS

ACKNOWLEDGEMENTS

I **WOULD LIKE** to thank the following people who helped proofread *Bumbling with the Arabs All the Way to the Bank*: Sheri Koshkin, Michael Koshkin, Sharon Alexander, Deanna Morey, Naomi Friedman, Brad Dill, David Schwarz, Dr. Harvey Klein, Mark Brookner, John Nugent, Rick Yarbrough, John Cates, Jerry Robbins, and Clayton Lee. Thank you also to Deborah Froese and River Chau of Indigo River Publishing for their creative suggestions throughout the editing process.

INTRODUCTION

I N 1980, MY former partner and I bumbled into a real estate deal with Ahmed Al Babtain, a billionaire from Kuwait. That deal consequently led to our completing over $250 million worth of business with the Arabs.

Mahmoud Al Adasani, formerly the undersecretary to the oil minister of Kuwait, became a close personal friend and was a welcomed guest who would stay two to three weeks at a time at our home in Houston. For four years, Mahmoud signed all the sales contracts to sell oil for the government of Kuwait; if Mahmoud didn't sign the contract, Kuwait didn't sell the oil. We were working with incredibly wealthy and powerful people from a culture very different from our own. Those differences were often startling, sometimes scary, and in many cases, they had humorous side effects. I was fortunate to experience and to see firsthand many things that most people would never experience in a hundred lifetimes.

Many of the businessmen we dealt with were above

the law in their respective countries as they were generally of royal lineage, oversaw or created the laws, and typically traveled on diplomatic passports. In one case, I was dealing with a person who drafted his country's constitution.

After every trip to the Middle East, we would have people with crew cuts wearing dark suits with thin ties and dark sunglasses flocking to our office. We had visits from the CIA, National Security Agency, US State Department, US Army, US Department of Defense, Israeli Mossad, Iranian Savak, British MI-6, French Military Intelligence, the Egyptian Armed Forces, and the Saudi Arabian General Intelligence Presidency (GIP), also known as the General Intelligence Directorate, the primary intelligence agency of the Kingdom of Saudi Arabia.

However, if I were an intelligence agent, I probably wouldn't use the name of the agency I worked for on my business card—and they probably didn't either!

My partner and I were involved in commercial real estate brokerage, the construction of single-family residential houses, and small residential land developments. During the first Persian Gulf War (1980–1988) while Iraq and Iran were fighting, a continuous stream of people visited our office wanting us to buy or arrange the purchase of an incredible variety of military weapons and armament. In many cases, these people were selling to both sides simultaneously. We had no interest in getting involved in the weapons business, but our partners in the Middle East kept recommending us.

When my partner and I began working together, we were two naïve, young Houston real estate go-getters who knew nothing about the Middle East other than where it was located on a world globe—on the side opposite the US. From our first encounter with Kuwaitis in 1980, we learned to navigate our relationships with the Arabs. And then, in 1989, a year after the first Persian Gulf War ended, I had a brilliant idea for a real estate deal in Iraq. I figured doing business in Iraq couldn't be much different than deal-making in Kuwait, right?

Under the umbrella of that adventuresome trip to Iraq, *Bumbling with the Arabs all the Way to the Bank* shares a number of stories from my encounters with Arabs—snapshots, if you will—of the different culture and attitudes that shaped my experience and broadened my world view.

The events described in this book are true as I remember them, but a few names have been changed for self-preservation concerns.

1

IRAQ TRIP: A BIG IDEA

DURING THE FIRST Persian Gulf War, Iraq and Iran staged continual artillery duels around the important Iraqi city of Basra in the southern area of the country, creating major devastation. The closest image I can compare it to is old World War II pictures showing piles of rubble—homes and retail and office buildings after the US B-29s had bombed them. When the war ended in 1988, the Iraqi government decided to clear out all the damaged buildings and property in Basra. After they finished, the city suddenly had over twenty-five thousand new home-building sites ready for construction.

With nineteen years of experience as a real estate broker—twelve of those years in land development and many of them with Arabs investing in US real estate—my interest was piqued. In 1989, I was in Houston, Texas, wondering how we could capitalize on the situation.

Suddenly, a lightbulb went off: *why don't we go over to Iraq and build a modular-home manufacturing plant to provide modular homes for expedited housing construction for thousands of Iraqi families?*

Modular homes, which are houses built in a factory and constructed on the building site in large pieces, seemed like the perfect solution. It would be a rapid and efficient way to provide major residential housing to quickly alleviate the housing shortage.

I'd been to Kuwait before to find money and partners for real estate deals. Most of the people I dealt with in Kuwait spoke better English than I did. They knew their way around Kuwait City like the back of their hand and were very knowledgeable about world affairs. They dressed well, and most had relatives or friends working in the government who could resolve problems quickly, understood what I said, and looking back, it seemed like they may have gone out of their way to try and help me.

How different could Iraq be?

I immediately called Mahmoud Al Adasani, the former undersecretary to the oil minister of Kuwait. I'd met him several years ago through business, and we became such good friends that he would stay at my house whenever he came to Houston.

Mahmoud's name is special in Kuwait. In fact,

Mahmoud Al Adasani has its own special kind of magic. On my first trip to Kuwait in 1982 Mahmoud said he would meet me at the airport.

I asked him, "Where do I meet you?"

He said, "Just ask for Mahmoud Al Adasani."

I thought that was strange, but I figured maybe they had a tiny airport and everybody would know everybody else.

So I had flown to Kuwait in August with no idea what I was doing—similar to my anticipated adventure in Iraq years later. When they opened the hatch door for me to get off the plane, I was slammed by a wave of heat. It felt like they were doing a pour in a steel blast furnace—which I had previously experienced from about fifty yards away at a GM automobile manufacturing plant in Hamtramck, Michigan. When they started the pour, you got hit by a tidal wave of air and the temperature instantly went up twenty degrees or more.

After exiting the plane, we walked down a ramp, across the tarmac, and then up a flight of stairs to enter the terminal. By the time I got to the air-conditioned space, I was soaked—like I had just jumped into a swimming pool.

What had I gotten myself into?

I didn't realize I needed a visa to get into Kuwait, so

I didn't have one. When the customs agent asked for my visa, I handed him my passport.

He said, "No, I need your visa."

"What visa?"

"The one you have to have to enter the country of Kuwait."

"I don't have one."

"Well, you can't enter Kuwait. We'll put you on the first flight back to the country you just came from."

I was in absolute shock. Then I stammered, "Mahmoud Al Adasani said he would take care of everything."

"Mahmoud Al Adasani in the Oil Ministry?"

"Yes."

The customs agent immediately stamped my passport, and someone led me to a private exit where Mahmoud was waiting for me.

Between that kind of respect for Mahmoud in Kuwait and the friendship we had developed over the years, you can see that it made sense for me to call Mahmoud about my Iraqi modular housing idea.

When I presented my plan to Mahmoud, he said, "Great idea, come on over!"

So I bought my ticket and reflected on my previous adventures with Arabs.

2

IT ALL BEGAN IN HOUSTON

THIS IS HOW it all began nine years before my trip to Iraq. My future partner—we'll call him Bill—and I met in 1980 through a mutual friend, Sam Plummer, who was a Houston homebuilder. Bill and I decided we wanted to do something together in business, but we didn't know what. At the time, Bill headed a home-building division for a regional homebuilder, and I had co-brokered one of the subdivisions he was building in, Parkhollow. I had a land development company that was developing Westhollow Village about a mile away. A brother of Bill's—we'll call him Mark— had purchased a home in Parkhollow, but Mark and his wife decided it was more house than they needed. So Mark put a sign in the yard that read: *For Sale By Owner.*

The following day, a realtor knocked on Mark's door and said he had someone who wanted to buy the home, but there was a problem. The buyers were Kuwaitis and wouldn't arrive in the US for three months.

Mark said, "Not a problem," and signed the earnest-money contract to sell the home.

About a month later, there was another knock at Mark's front door on a Thursday evening. He opened the door and there stood an attractive lady he didn't recognize. She wore a navy suit and looked to be in her late thirties or early forties. The lady said, "My name is Becky Petrina [pseudonym], and I'm here from Kuwait. My husband and I contracted to buy your home. I'm here early and wanted to know if we could close the sale of the home tonight."

Obviously, Becky did not understand the process to buy and sell real estate in Houston at the time. Mark told her that he and his wife would be happy to close the sale as soon as possible, but that it could take a week to get all the documentation together. He and his wife owned another vacant home, so they could move out very quickly.

Becky told Mark that her English wasn't that good and that she knew no one else in the US. She wanted to know if Mark and his wife would continue to live in the home as her guests until her husband arrived from Kuwait. Mark and his wife thought the request was unusual, but they agreed.

Every time Bill visited Mark, Becky would tell him that she and her husband were very well connected in Kuwait and that they wanted to do business with him. Becky was always going ten different ways at once at one hundred miles per hour. Many times when she spoke, you had no idea what she was talking about. She was absolutely the most scatterbrained person I had ever met! Every time I was around Becky, I could hear my mind saying, *Does not compute, does not compute!*

Since Becky was so flakey, all Bill could think about was how to leave gracefully and get away from her as quickly as possible. Eventually Becky's husband arrived in the US, and Mark and his wife moved out.

One Sunday during a Houston Oiler's football game, Becky called Bill and said he had to come over. She had friends in from Kuwait who wanted to do business with him. Feeling trapped, Bill agreed to go over to Becky's home after the football game.

The ballgame was over about three thirty, and when Bill got to the house, Becky took him into the den to meet six people, both men and women. She introduced everyone and told Bill these people wanted to do business with him in Houston.

Bill noticed that a couple of the women wore expensive-looking jewelry. The men appeared well groomed and wore nice clothes. Bill was still skeptical, but said to Becky, "How do I know the people here are financially capable?"

One of the men opened his wallet and showed Bill a slip for a million dollars that he had just deposited in a local Houston bank. A lady opened her purse and showed him a recent deposit slip for $950,000. Bill realized very quickly that there was enough money in the room to do something, but he wasn't sure what. He did not leave Becky's home until very late that night.

Becky wanted to create a partnership where she would set up the appointments in Kuwait, have Bill come over and introduce him as "my good friend Bill from the US, and you ought to invest your money with him." They would then split the profits.

As Bill left, he told Becky he would need to think about it for a few days. The next day Bill came by to tell me what had happened.

"I'm interested, but I'm not a broker," Bill told me, "so I can't get paid commissions for selling the Kuwaitis real estate. Would you be interested in doing this with me?"

We discussed it for a couple of hours and I thought about it. I knew Becky was a ten on the Flake Scale. The questions really boiled down to: Was she believable? Did she really have good money contacts in Kuwait? How much money would we have to invest, and how long would it take to start generating sufficient income to support the venture?

Because Becky was flakey as hell, we weren't sure about the answer to the first question. She seemed to have good money contacts; she had introduced Bill to people who supposedly had money and wanted to do real estate business with Bill. We decided that if we did go forward, we'd have to commit as much as $100,000 for up to six months to get the deal off and running.

I took a deep breath and said, "Okay, let's roll the dice."

We rented a small office space near San Felipe and Voss in Houston. The game plan was to go out and find at least three deals we could document and support with pictures in each of the real estate categories. If someone was interested in real estate, we wanted to have the waterfront covered.

It took us approximately ninety days, but we put together a huge presentation book that was probably eight inches thick. The book covered raw land for investment, land for subdivision development, land for apartments, and land for commercial properties. We had also developed single-family lots, single-family homes, existing apartments, existing retail and office space, and existing warehousing. We might have also included a townhome project or two.

We decided Bill would go to Kuwait and I would stay here in Houston. When Bill left for Kuwait, we didn't know if he would be able to sell the Kuwaitis any real estate, but we were assured that we had real estate investments available in every area of Houston that the investors might be interested in buying.

Bill left for a two week trip to Kuwait, and we met right after he got back. I asked, "How was the trip?"

"It was fantastic. I met the secretary of defense, the president of the National Bank of Kuwait, and a whole bunch of important people."

"How much real estate did you sell?"

"Nothing, but I did meet a lot of impressive people."

I was really disappointed and ready to close down the operation. Bill pleaded not to and said he thought he could get some deals done on the next trip. One of the real problems we faced was that we had used up almost all of the $100 grand and I was almost personally tapped out. Where would we get the money for another trip? I told Bill I wanted to think about it and we would talk the next day.

That night I did some serious thinking about the whole deal. Had we just pissed off a hundred grand? Could we make the deal work? Was Becky helping or not?

The next morning, I checked my credit card balances,

and I still had nearly $10,000 available on one of my credit cards. That was more than enough to pay for a trip to Kuwait and the associated expenses. The real question was: *am I getting ready to throw good money after bad?*

I finally decided that because we already had so much time and money invested, it was worth another try. I told Bill I would put up the money if he gave me his word that he would do something for me. I told him I was uncomfortable with Becky, and I was sure she was perceived to be flakey by Kuwaiti standards. I told Bill I wanted his promise that he would spend part of his time in Kuwait away from Becky, trying to sell some real estate on his own. He promised he would. A couple of weeks later Bill went back to Kuwait.

Now, what I'm getting ready to tell you is one hundred eighty degrees opposite of what actually happened. To help illustrate the context of what my partner and I experienced, I will give you this scenario:

Let's say you are a Kuwaiti who has a really good real estate deal in Kuwait, and you think there is a lot of money in the US. You fly to Dallas, Texas and go downtown. You're standing on the street corner looking at all the tall buildings in awe, like you are completely lost. A stranger notices this and walks up to you and asks if he can help you because you look lost and appear to be a foreigner.

You say, "I'm from Kuwait, and I have an excellent real estate investment there. I heard there are a lot of moneyed people in Texas who are looking for good investments, so I came to Dallas."

The stranger says, "You need to go speak to Trammel Crow."

"Who is Trammel Crow?"

"He is the largest real estate developer in the US."

"I'd like to meet him, but I don't know where his office is."

"Trammel Crow offices in that building over there," the stranger says, pointing at a tall building.

You say, "Thank you," and go to the building where Trammel Crow has his offices.

You see his name in the building directory, go to his office, and ask the receptionist to see Trammel Crow. You don't know how, but you get inside to see Trammel Crow in person. You give him your five-minute sales presentation.

Afterward, Trammel Crow gets up from behind his desk, walks over to you, puts his hand on your shoulder, and says, "Son, I like the way you handle yourself. I'll tell you what I will do. I'll put up one hundred percent of the money and we will split the profits fifty-fifty."

Well, you are so high, you probably don't even need an airplane to fly back to Kuwait.

About two months later you go back to Dallas to have Trammel Crow sign all the legal documents to close the transaction.

Trammel Crow looks at the documents and says, "I can't sign these."

Your heart goes clunk as it falls.

You say, "Why? It was such a good deal."

Trammel Crow says, "No, I believed you that it was a good deal. In fact, I thought it was so good that I sold part of my interest to some of my friends."

You don't recognize the strange American names because they have last names like Kennedy, DuPont, Rockefeller, Ford, and Hunt. You know that Trammel Crow is supposedly wealthy, so you have the closing documents redrawn and hope the deal will close. As it turns out, the deal closes, as do many more after that.

So that is what happened to us and how we started doing real estate deals in Kuwait and then the whole Arabian Peninsula. It was pure blind luck when we bumbled into a deal with a billionaire, Ahmed Al Babtain, one of the "who's who" from the Middle East who became our partners.

A $2,500 LUNCH

My partner Bill met Ahmed Al Babtain in Kuwait in

1980 when we were doing our first real estate deal. All I knew about Ahmed at the time was that he owned some automobile dealerships in Kuwait, he had enough money to do a deal with us, and our first closing had gone very smoothly.

I met Ahmed for the first time in Houston in 1981. I was surprised to see him wearing casual Western clothes. He was about five feet ten, probably weighed 180 pounds, and had some facial hair. It would be hard to describe the facial hair as a beard; it was more like an unshaven goatee. Ahmed's spoken English was not good, but I learned very quickly that normally he had excellent comprehension of what was being said.

Ahmed was coming to Houston for the first time, and we wanted to make a good impression. At that point my partner and I were broke, but we wanted to take Ahmed out to an impressive restaurant. We finally decided to take him to Ruth's Chris Steak House.

I was a few minutes late, but it wasn't a problem. As it turned out, Ahmed had a friend with him. After introductions, we all looked at the menu and ordered steaks.

Our server then asked, "Would you like to see our wine list?"

Before I could say anything, Ahmed said, "Bring us a bottle of your most expensive wine."

Holy shit! We were using one of my credit cards to pay for this! I wasn't sure of my available credit, but I thought I had $2,000, maybe $2,500, left. I had no idea how much the most expensive bottle of wine that Ahmed had just ordered was going to cost me. I was very uncomfortable but kept smiling and continued the small talk.

The wine steward opened the bottle, poured some for Ahmed, and asked if he liked the wine. Ahmed said it was delicious and ordered another bottle!

My butt cheeks were clenched so tight, it's a wonder I didn't pull a muscle in my caboose right there. I was numb. It was Heart Attack City. I had no idea how much two bottles of the most expensive wine in the house would cost, but it was probably more than my credit card could handle.

We talked about different things, but all I could think about was the embarrassment there would be when my credit card was declined, and we couldn't pay the bill. I truly don't remember anything discussed at that meal. Ahmed and his friend decided they wanted coffee. When the bill finally came, the total was $2,200 without tip. I handed our waiter my credit card and took a deep breath. About five of the longest damned minutes of my life passed before the waiter returned with the bill and my credit card. I had visions of screwing up our relationship with a wealthy Arab before it had even started!

I opened the little leather folder with my credit card and saw the bill. The waiter didn't say anything. I couldn't believe it! The charge hadn't been declined. I had trouble picking up the pen because my hand was actually shaking; I had to steady it with my other hand. Hopefully, no one noticed. Normally I am a big tipper, but I put down 12 percent. That made the lunch bill for four people in 1981 a total of $2,464!

As I went out the front door I promised God I would amend my wicked ways. Later I called for my credit card balance. Five dollars and change left in available credit. Absolutely unbelievable!

PLANNED CITIES CONTRACTS

On Ahmed Al Babtain's second trip to Houston to meet with us later that same year, there was a major surprise. Although we had completed one deal with Ahmed and had another deal under contract, he was still an unknown entity. We were very aware that we were dealing with someone from a different country that had different cultural values.

Ahmed came to our offices one afternoon with something he wanted to show us: two books about the size of the New York City white pages. They were two signed contracts—one signed by the government of Saudi Arabia and the other by the government of Libya—to build two new cities.

Ahmed said he had signed the contracts and was willing to sell them to us for a five percent premium with nothing down. He would just assign them to us.

At that point in time my partner and I were small real estate brokers, builders, and developers in Houston. We were overwhelmed. We told Ahmed we would need to study the contracts and get back to him. As it turned out, my partner was going to be tied up most of the next day with San Jacinto Savings on a complicated real estate deal we were working on to buy over two hundred homes scattered throughout Houston, so I took the material home to review.

That evening, I started to go through the first contract from Saudi Arabia. I could not believe what I was reading. Ahmed really did have a signed contract to build a whole fricking city! It looked like half the officials in Saudi Arabia had signed the document. This is not exact, but it gives you an idea of the magnitude of the contract. It was a proposal to build the following:

- thirty-three schools from primary (elementary) to college level
- fifteen hospitals

- twelve governmental buildings
- twelve mosques
- twenty-five large parks
- two major power plants plus the major transmission lines to serve a city of 100,000 people
- sanitary sewer plants to service 100,000 people
- water wells and water plants to service 100,000 people
- all the streets and utility lines to develop a city for 100,000 people
- twenty thousand apartment units
- approximately 17,500 single-family homes for 70,000 people
- retail shopping centers
- office buildings
- five major industrial parks
- port facilities
- rail lines and terminals

Now let's compare the size of that contract to our company's stature. Our company had built two hundred new single-family residential homes that year. If we were contracted to build only the single-family residential homes listed, it would have taken us eighty-seven and a half years to complete at our current building rate. And that list was only a very small portion of the overall contract.

It was beyond anything I had ever dreamed of in real estate, and I was looking at a signed contract that was offered to us with nothing down! We're talking about a cost-plus contract for billions and *billions* of dollars.

I then looked at the other contract, which was similar but a little smaller. Unbelievable! My partner and I met the next day to discuss the contract. I told Bill these contracts were so far out of our league, he couldn't imagine. I recommended that he take them home that night and take a look himself. The following day we got together again, and he likened it to someone who could drive an eighteen-foot speedboat suddenly being put in charge of the Queen Mary.

As appealing as the opportunity was, there was no way we could complete the contract. Even if we had taken the contract to Brown & Root—at the time, I think, the largest civil engineering company in the world—they would have needed to go out and get additional partners to have done a deal of such magnitude.

The bottom line was we passed, but it was another interesting day dealing with the Arabs. And there were lots more interesting days to come.

SALIM'S BANK IN FRANCE

One afternoon, about six months after we completed

our first deal with Ahmed Al Babtain, I was in the office when the receptionist said there was a very young man who wanted to see me. He said Ahmed had recommended us.

I told the receptionist, "Send him on back."

The young man came into my office and introduced himself as Salim. Salim was not the first person Ahmed had recommended to us, but he was the youngest. (Over time, Ahmed and other Arabs from wealthy families sent a steady stream of people our way.)

I asked, "What can I do for you?"

He told me he wanted to buy a newer office building in Houston. "I've got $10 million to invest."

"There are numerous opportunities in Houston. Please forgive me for asking, but you look very young. How old are you?"

"I am twenty-eight."

I was thinking, *I'm really not sure if he's not thirteen.* I asked him, "Do you plan on buying the building for cash, or will you need financing?"

"Cash."

I asked, "Do you have a preference for an area of town?"

"It doesn't matter, as long as it is a good deal."

I said, "Could I please get a contact name and

telephone number to verify proof of funds?"

"No problem." He then proceeded to give me the name of a bank in France, a contact name, and a telephone number.

I let him know I would be back to him with my recommendations within a week.

After he left, I thought to myself, *I don't know a soul in France, and I definitely don't speak French.* For about thirty minutes, I fretted back and forth with the idea of hiring someone who spoke fluent French to interpret the call I wanted to make to the French banker. Finally I decided, what the hell, I'd call myself. So I dialed the bank's number directly and asked for the contact that had been given to me. A man answered. I asked for the person who had been recommended at the bank.

In perfect English he said, "This is he."

I then introduced myself and explained that a young man had recently come to my office in Houston. He was interested in buying a Houston-area office building for $10 million in cash and had given me this name to verify he was financially capable.

Suddenly, there was laughter on the other end of the line. "Mr. Koshkin, are you aware of the size of our bank?"

I said no. I had absolutely no idea.

"Thirty-six billion francs on deposit."

That meant absolutely nothing to me because I didn't know the exchange rate for francs and dollars.

The banker said, "The exchange rate is about six francs to the dollar."

I did some quick math and determined that the bank had the equivalent of $6 billion in deposits, making it larger than any bank in Houston.

He then asked, "Do you know how many stockholders there are in our bank?"

I had no idea and responded, "No."

"One, and it is the person who recommended that you call me."

"I guess that means he's financially capable."

More laughter on the phone as he responded, "Yes, he is financially capable. By the way, if you do not know it, I am the president of the bank."

"That works for me. Thank you for your time." Then I hung up.

It was truly fairyland. Surprise! We ended up doing a deal with Salim.

AHMED'S OIL LEASE

Ahmed Al Babtain did not speak English very well, but his comprehension was excellent. One afternoon during his second visit to Houston, Ahmed came into my office because he needed help. By that time, we had successfully completed two land deals with Ahmed, and we were starting to feel a little more comfortable dealing with him. Ahmed often spoke of deals that were off the charts, and we didn't know if he was just trying to impress us with big deals or if he really was that well connected and did these large deals all the time.

I asked, "What kind of help do you need?"

"Oil."

I told him I wasn't in the oil business and was not that knowledgeable about oil, but I would try to help. "What do you need?"

Ahmed then produced an letter-sized sheet of white paper with a drawing on it in black. I looked at it and couldn't make out heads or tails of what I was looking at. "What is this?"

He replied, "An oil lease."

With oil production common throughout the state of Texas, I assumed the map was a copy of some oil lease Ahmed had gotten into in the area. There was not a scale on the drawing denoting size, and no roads were shown. So I asked Ahmed, "What is the size?"

"Fifty-seven million hectares."

I had no idea how big a hectare was and tried to get Ahmed to explain it to me. We went back and forth for ten minutes trying to understand each other. Finally, he asked if I had seen his big boat. Yes, I'd seen his big boat. He told me it would do about twenty miles per hour. He then motioned to the paper from one side of the drawing to the other.

I nodded.

He said, "One and a half days to get from one end to the other."

With some quick calculations, it appeared that Ahmed's oil lease was 720 miles long by 300 miles wide. I was in shock. I still didn't know where the oil lease was, but I knew it was huge—about 216,000 square miles. Now, our discussion had already taken half an hour, and I still didn't have a clue where the oil lease was.

I looked at the map again and I noticed Mindanao. "Is the lease in the Philippines?"

Ahmed lit up like a Christmas tree. "Yes!"

Terrific! At least I had located the area of the oil lease. We were making progress. After thinking about it for a minute, I figured the oil lease was probably twice as large as the whole land area of the Philippine Islands. Then it dawned on me why Ahmed had brought up his big boat: the picture I was looking at was not land, but water. The whole lease was for offshore oil. The lease was incredibly large, about 35 percent of the total size of the Gulf of

Mexico. It was so large that it would probably take a consortium of a half dozen of the largest oil companies in the world to drill the lease during our lifetime!

I told Ahmed I probably couldn't help him because we really didn't have those types of oil contacts.

It was something new every day, and you can be assured if Ahmed was involved, it was really big.

MEETING MAHMOUD AL ADASANI

I'm sure at one time or another, most people in business have experienced one of those weeks when everything is on overload. In early 1981, I was enduring one of those weeks. By Thursday afternoon, I already felt like pulling my hair out, and Friday's schedule was a killer. That morning, I was in the office early to prepare for the day's meetings. The receptionist buzzed me to tell me I had a guest. I asked who it was.

She said his name was—and she spelled it—Mahmoud Al Adasani. "And his business card says he is the undersecretary to the oil minister of Kuwait."

I didn't know him, but typically, most of the people I had previously met with big titles from foreign countries were in charge of the broom closet.

"Ahmed Al Babtain said he needed to speak to you."

Those were the magic words. "Send him back."

Mahmoud came in and introduced himself. He was wearing the traditional white *dishdasha* that most men from the Middle East wear, Arab garb that looks like pajamas. He was heavyset, about five feet ten and two hundred pounds, had graying dark hair, and wore sandals and large, black, horn-rimmed glasses. He said he had a real estate problem, and Ahmed Al Babtain had said I could probably solve the problem.

I said I would try—all the while thinking this clown needed to be out of my office within ten minutes or I was going to be late to my first appointment of a very long day.

As Mahmoud started to explain the problem, I realized it was not going to be a quick fix I could handle by myself. I was going to have to get Larry Milberger or Dick Miller of R.G. Miller Engineers involved, and probably Pepe Schwartz of Schwartz, Page & Harding—Municipal Utility District attorneys—along with the City of Houston Engineering Department, and possibly the head of Public Works for the City of Houston. Given that Ahmed had recommended me, I didn't want to let him down.

I told Mahmoud to call me in the early afternoon. Mahmoud left, and I begrudgingly canceled all my meetings for the whole day and started calling people. When Mahmoud called back later, I was still up to my rear in alligators. I told him we were working on it and to try me about four thirty.

When Mahmoud came back at four thirty I told him everything had been worked out.

He asked, "How much?"

I said, "There's no charge." All I really wanted was for him to leave and not come back.

He said, "Thank you." Then he left.

I did not hear from him for a year. In fact, it was almost a year to the day when he came back to my office. I thought, *Oh no, not again.* Mahmoud explained his real estate problem, and luckily it had a simple solution. I made a quick call to Larry Milberger, and the problem was resolved while Mahmoud was still in my office.

Mahmoud asked, "How much?"

I said, "No charge."

Mahmoud thanked me and left.

Years later, as we became good friends, I found out I was the only one who never charged him for services—all because I just wanted him out of my office.

Maybe that's why he was so willing to help years later when I had the big Iraq idea about modular homes.

3

COURTING THE ARABS

GETTING TO KNOW Ahmed Al Babtain threw Bill and me into a truly unfamiliar world and it connected us with a bunch of other Arab businessmen. We were in for our fair share of adventure and we learned a lot about courting the Arabs as friends and business associates.

About a year-and-a-half after meeting Ahmed, he announced that he wanted to host a party at his new Clear Lake house for some of his friends. (More about the Clear Lake real estate deal later!) We asked how many people he was talking about. He guessed maybe three hundred or so, and he wanted our help in planning the shindig.

Bill and I discussed how much we should budget for the party. After fifteen minutes of bouncing back and forth, we decided that $25 to $35 per head would be conservative. So we had a couple of secretaries plan out something with a budget of $10,000. We then presented the budget to Ahmed.

After he looked at it for a few minutes, Ahmed said, "You know, I really wanted to have a little nicer party."

I asked, "How much nicer?"

He said, "One hundred thousand dollars!"

"Dollars?"

"Yes."

"How are you possibly going to spend that much on a party?"

Little did we know. In the end, Ahmed actually ended up spending a little over $160,000 on the party! Now, how did Ahmed spend $160,000 on the party? Here's a breakdown:

Fly in ten-piece band and their equipment from Saudi Arabia	$18,000
Fly in three belly dancers from Kuwait	4,000
Fly in a dozen Scandinavian ladies from Scandinavia	9,600
Fly in two chefs from Kuwait	2,400
Food	18,000
Liquor and drinks	18,000
Gift bags for the guests	27,500
Hotel, food, and miscellaneous for fifty guests	20,000
Fees for band, belly dancers, and ladies	25,000
Limo rentals	10,000
Miscellaneous	7,500
TOTAL ESTIMATED PARTY COST	**$160,000**

If we hadn't been involved, I wouldn't have believed it.

Since this little party had morphed from a small $10,000 party to a $160,000 extravaganza, some of our people had gotten really hyped. One of our secretaries, who was a skydiver, asked my partner and me if we would pay for a plane rental so she and two friends could skydive into the party.

Bill said, "Sure, let's do it."

Obviously, we were boarding a runaway freight train. What could go wrong?

The night of the party, the three skydivers had boarded the plane but were concerned about the crosswinds that had been swirling before takeoff. Their intent was to land on the street in front of Ahmed's house. As the plane buzzed overhead, the people who had gotten to the party early all came outside to watch. Everything went just as planned. The girls jumped, the colorful parachutes opened, and they glided down in a large, looping circle. Amazing—except they had miscalculated the wind and ended up in the water 150 yards from shore!

Luckily, there was a twenty-foot fishing boat tied up at the dock. Ron Peek, one of our brokers and head of our retail operation, and another person hopped into the boat and went to fish the girls out of the drink.

Their landing was a harbinger of things to come.

The girls, obviously, were drenched and had not

brought a change of clothes. Luckily, Ahmed had three pair of men's shorts and t-shirts they could use. So the girls showered and then joined the party. That is, they were barefooted wearing shorts with t-shirt tops and no bras.

Yeah, nobody would notice.

Our secretaries had agreed to act as servers for drinks, snacks, and food. I've got to admit, they were an impressive group of good-looking women. They did a great job, with the exception of two secretaries who had one too many and spilled drinks on guests. Of course, one of those guests was a Saudi prince who was a first cousin to the emir—the ruler of Saudi Arabia. He got a full glass of red wine down the front of his suit. Just our way of trying to impress everybody! Another man—who I think was the president of Royal Jordanian Airlines—also had a drink poured on him. We definitely made a lasting impression on a lot of people.

The band was okay. They played mostly Middle Eastern music with a pretty good beat. The belly dancers were outstanding! They were attractive, seductive, and really knew how to shake their booties.

One of the belly dancers, a real firecracker, looked like a contortionist with some of her moves. Her shaking suggested that she had worn out more than a few men in bed. I don't think that I could have made it past the second inning with her if my life depended upon it.

The people my partner and I invited included our lenders along with other lenders we wanted to do business with, some of our larger contractors, our engineers, and local politicians who could be helpful on future business deals. Ahmed invited friends and business partners from the Middle East and Europe.

I didn't meet everybody at the party, but all the people I did meet seemed to have more money than God. Most owned a string of companies similar to a conglomerate on the New York Stock Exchange! They were businessmen providing goods and services to the royal families throughout the Middle East. A few people from Europe attended, including the president of Mercedes Benz—he may have been president of their European operations—whom I spoke to briefly. I think there were people from Kuwait, Saudi Arabia, Dubai, Abu Dhabi, Yemen, Algeria, and Jordan. A number of these guests were members of the royal families of these countries. I don't remember if anyone from Egypt, Syria, Oman, Iran, or Iraq was there. At that time Iran and Iraq were still at war.

Through all of our dealings in the Middle East over a ten-year period, only once did I ever see any of the people we were dealing with doing drugs.

With just one exception. Yup, you guessed it! It was at

Ahmed's party.

Three princes from Saudi Arabia were using a water pipe in one of the bedrooms. It was Ahmed's party, so I couldn't just go in and tell them to stop. I prayed that neither of the police chiefs from the City of Nassau Bay and the City of Houston went into the bedroom.

My wife, Sheri, and I were tired and left shortly before midnight. We heard later that at about one a.m. the girls from Scandinavia came out buck naked. The party really started rocking and rolling after that. Apparently, a couple of our overzealous secretaries joined in. Some of the guys told me later, it was the most unbelievable thing they had ever experienced in their lives. And these guys weren't Boy Scouts. They said it was ten times better than going to any strip club. By a stroke of luck, all the invited law enforcement people had already left the party.

Timing is everything.

For days afterward, I had visions of having to bail everybody out at four or five in the morning and suffering the international political headlines that would have resulted.

BUYING A GIFT FOR AHMED

When Ahmed decided to host that very expensive party at his new Clear Lake home, Bill and I fretted about the right housewarming gift for days. We considered buying Ahmed an ornate saddle, but we didn't know if he rode horses. If he did, he hadn't mentioned it to us. We wondered about a custom-made pair of Blackjack boots, but we had never seen him wear anything other than sandals. We thought of custom leather furniture, but Ahmed had purchased the home with all the furniture intact. A nice leather custom briefcase might have been a good idea, but we had never seen Ahmed carry a briefcase. A large houseplant was a *maybe*, but if Ahmed wasn't there, who would water it?

Finally, I suggested a bottle of expensive vintage Dom Pérignon champagne. After we settled on the champagne, instead of sending one bottle, Bill sent a whole over-the-top case at a cost of almost $1,400. At first, I was upset about the expenditure, but the more I thought about the situation, the more I realized my partner was right to send a whole case.

I kept thinking that champagne was nice but it wasn't a personal gift; I wanted to give Ahmed something personal. I went to an exclusive hat shop and bought him a grey Stetson cowboy hat with his initials embroidered on the front and sides of the hat—another quick $700, but it was unique.

The night of the party everything was going along

great when I presented the hat to Ahmed. Two young Saudis we had just done a real estate deal with stood beside him. When the applause stopped, Ahmed put the hat on and there was more clapping. Then Ahmed took the hat off and placed it on the head of one of the Saudis, who wore the hat the rest of the night. I would guess Ahmed wore the hat for a total of forty-five seconds.

Damn! I could have bought him a fountain pen or a ball cap.

COWBOY CLOTHES FOR AHMED

About a year later, Bill and I decided to get Ahmed some Western wear as a gift to show our gratitude for his friendship and business. We went to Stelzig's Western Wear. My partner and I aren't into Western wear but would occasionally dress up in Western style around our Arabic visitors.

We were met at the door by a perky, attractive saleslady who asked what we were looking for. We told her we wanted an outfit for a good client of ours. This sales lady had obviously seen us coming and knew we didn't know jack about Western wear.

She showed us long-sleeved Western shirts first. After looking at a couple dozen shirts, she recommended one that was only $80. Remember, this was the 1980s, and eighty bucks was a lot. We then looked at some pants. I thought we were going to buy Levi jeans. But *nooo!* She recommended some cockamamie Western pants at $200 a pair.

We then looked at belts. We found some nice leather belts in the $10 to $20 range, but by the time we added a custom-made belt buckle, it was $300. We had now spent almost $600, and we hadn't purchased boots or a hat. The boots ended up being Luccheses and cost $500. The hat was a Stetson that cost $300. With tax, we spent almost $1,500 for one Western-wear outfit.

The good news was that Ahmed appeared to like the gifts.

But unfortunately, neither of us ever saw him wear the outfit.

MY PARTNER'S BIRTHDAY PARTY

One year, Bill's girlfriend spent three or four weeks planning a surprise birthday party for him. At the last minute, Ahmed flew into Houston, so he was invited. The party was a typical barbecue with birthday cake. After the cake was eaten, Bill opened the birthday gifts. He received the normal types of gifts you would expect, like fishing gear, hunting equipment, and items for the office. But one gift that stood out as a little bit unusual.

When my partner opened the gift from Ahmed, he found a kilo bar of pure gold. At the time it was probably worth $20 grand. Since everything about dealing with the Arabs was over the top, my partner decided to use the 2.2-pound gold bar as a doorstop at his ranch house! It was well used for many years.

FISHING WITH MAHMOUD

I've always been an avid fisherman, and during the 1980s I usually booked three to six guided fishing trips with Blaien Friermood, an expert fishing guide in the Houston area. Blaien was a good friend and a real hot dog. The first time I went fishing with him, we went to the Galveston Bay complex where he helped a buddy of mine and me catch our limit real quick. My buddy also caught an enormous speckled trout—the biggest caught that year in the entire area, including Trinity Bay. In fact, if the fish had been entered in any Galveston Bay fishing tournament that year, it would have won, hands down.

About six months later, I scheduled another fishing trip with Blaien. Since Mahmoud had just come to town, I asked him if he would like to go fishing.

Mahmoud replied, "Sure."

I couldn't believe it because I knew he wasn't a fisherman or an early riser. But I immediately called Blaien and asked, "How's the fishing been?"

"It's been lousy."

I told Blaien I had invited Mahmoud Al Adasani, the undersecretary to the oil minister of Kuwait, to go fishing with us. I asked, "Is there any way you can guarantee a great fishing trip?"

Blaien chuckled and replied, "Ben, you grew up fishing and are one of the more knowledgeable fishing clients that I have. The tides are at the wrong times, the wind has been blowing like crazy, the bay isn't salty enough, and the water in parts of the bay is off-color. That was a really dumb question on your part." He suggested that I cancel the trip.

I refused.

Blaien said, "Okay. Remember to bring some Vietnamese sandwiches, and don't expect to catch many fish."

I always brought Vietnamese sandwiches along on fishing trips. Made with a French baguette, they had a butter-mayonnaise spread, grated carrots, a cucumber slice, cilantro, a thin slice of jalapeño, seasoned salt, and soy sauce with ham, chicken, barbecued pork, or meatballs.

Mahmoud and I got up at 4:30 a.m. to get ready. Mahmoud usually went to bed very late, and he looked bleary-eyed, so I told him he could sleep on the drive. He woke up when we met Blaien at six a.m. We were in the water heading for the first honey hole in less than a half hour. It felt great to be out on the water, but I knew it would get hotter than hell later that morning. If the wind picked up, we would be more comfortable but the water would be too rough to catch fish in some of the best spots. If the wind didn't pick up, we would melt in the heat but we could fish some of the better spots.

Blaien said, "Ben, I know you like to fish with artificials, but the fish have been running deeper, so we're going to use live bait. We'll use shrimp, and if we see one of the shrimpers I'm looking for, we'll get some baby croakers. We'll fish with popping corks about five feet deep."

At our first stop, we caught half a dozen small specs within fifteen minutes, but we only kept three that were legal size. Thankfully, Mahmoud appeared to be enjoying himself.

But then Blaien said, "Reel 'em in boys 'cause the big ones aren't here." He took us to another stop. We eased in near a gas well and drifted over the shell pad that attracted smaller fish. Those, in turn, attracted bigger fish. We quickly caught a few small fish, mostly throwbacks.

Blaien pointed to a boat in the distance and said, "There's the shrimper I've been watching for. Reel 'em in."

We reeled in our lines and pulled alongside the shrimp boat, where Blaien bought two dozen live croakers. Then we headed for an area toward the middle of Trinity Bay, but as we approached, the wind started to pick up and the water got rougher. Mahmoud clutched his seat tightly. We slowed down, and after a few slow passes, Blaien found an area to anchor.

Blaien said, "We are fishing near a small wreck on a sandy bottom. If the specs are here, they will absolutely blast the croakers. There will be no doubt when you get a hit."

We rigged up using live croakers and cast our lines. For fifteen minutes, the waves bounced us around. We caught nothing. Nada. Mahmoud looked pretty uncomfortable the whole time. He said, "Let's go back to one of those first spots where we were catching fish."

But just then, I got our first real strike. It took a few minutes to net the three-and-a-half-pound spec. It was a nice chunky fish. Then Mahmoud and Blaien both caught fish on at the same time.

Mahmoud looked a little happier and said, "I need some help."

I told him, "Keep the rod tip up."

He did, and Blaien netted Mahmoud's fish, which was about five pounds—an excellent spec. Blaien had lost a fish to help Mahmoud but immediately got another strike. The action continued for about an hour until we had caught four barely legal fish and ten nice ones ranging from two and a half pounds to almost six pounds.

By the time we'd made our haul, the water had grown too rough to fish. And by that time, Mahmoud really didn't look well. He said, "I think I'm getting seasick."

It took us almost a half hour of rough riding before we got to sheltered water, and Mahmoud clutched his seat the entire way.

Blaien said, "Let's break out the Vietnamese sandwiches."

Mahmoud, who still looked a little green, said he wasn't hungry. But by the time Blaien and I started chowing down sandwiches and cold drinks, he changed his mind and asked for a sandwich.

I asked, "What type do you want?"

Mahmoud had never had a Vietnamese sandwich. As he was reaching for one, I suddenly remembered the barbecued pork. Mahmoud didn't eat pork! I quickly handed him a chicken sandwich and a coke, saying "I brought chicken for you."

After taking a couple of bites, Mahmud said, "You know, this is a pretty good sandwich."

Good thing he hadn't grabbed the pork.

After we finished eating, Blaien said, "Let's go catch some reds." He cranked up the motor and took us to an area that looked like a big drainage ditch with ten foot high spoil banks on either side. The good news? The banks cut the wind down dramatically. We were fishing with shrimp again.

Mahmoud said, "My cork is moving, but it's not going under."

Blaien said, "It's probably a flounder. Let it continue to mouth the bait, and wait for it to slowly take it under before you set the hook."

About five minutes later Mahmoud caught his first flounder. As Blaien held it up, Mahmoud studied it and said, "It sure is a weird-looking fish."

Blaien smiled and said, "It may be weird looking, but they are really good eating."

We fished there for another hour, and Blaien caught two reds. Then Mahmoud caught his first red and said, "I don't feel well again. Can we head back?"

We decided to call it a day. As Blaien cleaned the fish later, I thanked him for another good trip under trying conditions and paid him, including a nice tip.

That night Sheri fixed speckled trout and redfish for Mahmoud. He was a happy camper and enjoyed his meal, but he never asked to go fishing again.

DUCK HUNTING WITH MAHMOUD

In November every year I used to take a group out for a weekend where we drank, played cards, ate, and went duck hunting. I typically invited lenders, contractors, and suppliers who had helped us during the year, as well as three or four of our employees who had performed well. Normally, we had about twenty people, so I would lease a hunting lodge for the weekend and hire one hunting guide for each four-man party. Naturally, Blaien was my guide.

The year after my fishing trip with Mahmoud, about a dozen people had accepted my invitation to go duck hunting. As the weekend approached, I got a call from Mahmoud.

He asked, "How are you doing?"

"Great," I said, "but it's been too long since I've seen you."

"That's why I'm calling. I'll be in Houston Friday about noon. I wanted to know if you could pick me up at Intercontinental Airport, and do you have room for me for about three weeks?"

"You're always welcome at our house, and we have room, but I've got a conflict. I've invited a group of guys to go duck hunting this weekend."

At this point, you need to be aware that virtually all

the Arabs we dealt with drank, smoked, gambled, and chased women, but none of them hunted. So I asked Mahmoud if he wanted to go, confident that he would say *no* because most Arabs didn't hunt.

But Mahmoud replied, "I'd love to go."

"Great," I said. At the same time I was thinking, *oh no!* Cold and possibly wet weather, the presence of guns, and the fact that Mahmoud was not a gun person *or* a morning person all added up to unbelievably bad luck for me!

That created a bunch of problems. The first was how to keep a group of drunken, partying SOBs from bringing up anything pertaining to Israel and the Arabs or offending Mahmoud in any way. The second issue was how to guarantee a great hunt. The third was getting waders and hunting clothes that fit Mahmoud. The fourth was inviting the rest of the people on my list. The fifth problem was calling all the people I had already invited and explaining the new situation about Mahmoud. The sixth was that I needed to complete some business before we left Friday afternoon. And the seventh problem was that I had to tell Sheri that Mahmoud would be staying with us for three to four weeks starting Sunday night.

It was only Wednesday afternoon, so I had plenty of time.

Wrong!

I suddenly found myself in a major time bind.

After getting off the phone with Mahmoud, the first thing I did was call Blaien Friermood, my friend and the expert guide who had taken Mahmoud and me fishing. I thought he was the best duck hunting guide in the Houston area. I had hunted with Blaien for years, and at one time I was his largest booker of duck hunts.

I told Blaien that we had to absolutely guarantee Mahmoud a great hunt.

He said, "The only way you're going to be able to do that is to stake out some domestic ducks to use if the hunt is slow, but the Feds would bury us under the jail if they caught us."

I told him, "Go do it. I'll pay any fine if we get caught."

He said he'd try to locate some ducks, but he wasn't sure he could do it under such extremely short notice.

The second thing I did was start calling everyone who said they were coming to explain that they had to be on good behavior because of Mahmoud and that I did not want the subject of Israel or the Arabs mentioned the complete weekend, period.

I then called my wife and said, "Mahmoud is coming to our house on Sunday evening and he'll being staying with us for a few weeks."

Sheri promptly hit me with a list of "Honey dos" that

I hadn't done. Not the least of which were a cracked window from a rock sent airborne by the grass mower, a dishwasher that was not working properly, and a ceiling fan broken by a football thrown by one of our kids.

I asked, "How bad is the ceiling fan?"

Sheri said, "It's hanging by one wire and it's *catawampus*." In other words, she thought it was totaled.

"I'll get it taken care of."

I immediately called one of our employees who happened to be a very good handyman. I told him to fix everything on my wife's list and replace the fan and light kit by Saturday at the latest.

He said, "I will try."

"No," I told him. "Trying isn't an option. I want it done to my wife's satisfaction by Saturday, or everything will hit the fan. The undersecretary to the oil minister of Kuwait will be at our house on Sunday and staying with us for three or four weeks."

Without a whole lot of enthusiasm, he agreed to get it done.

The next morning, I called another of one our employees who was an avid hunter, someone I thought would know what to buy to completely outfit Mahmoud for the hunt. The good news was that Mahmoud and I were approximately the same height and weight. Since I didn't know Mahmoud's shoe size, I told my employee to buy four pairs of waders in sizes 9, 10, 11, and 12, and get a number of pairs of socks that ranged from size 7 to 12. If Mahmoud had a smaller foot than size 9, he could put on multiple pairs of socks as needed to fit his feet in the waders.

Incredibly, everything fell into place. I told my partner, Bill, "I need the limo from late Friday morning until Monday morning." That was no problem since he was also going on the same duck hunt.

As it turned out, the work I needed to complete took less time than anticipated. By Friday morning I was thinking, *Boy, it looks like I've got it under control and maybe everything will work out okay.*

The game plan was to pick up Mahmoud at the airport and go directly to the hunting lodge ahead of all my guests so that I could make sure everything was in order. I figured we could be at the hunting lodge by 3:00 p.m. if all went well. I still had one nagging concern; I hadn't heard from Blaien about the live ducks he needed to buy.

What is it they say? *The best laid plans of mice and men . . .*

At about noon on Friday, I took our limo to the Houston Intercontinental Airport to pick up Mahmoud. Unfortunately, there was a major delay because of a large tropical storm. Mahmoud was about an hour and a half late. No problem. We still had time to get to the hunting lodge ahead of everyone else. But Mahmoud was not a good air traveler. When I greeted him at the gate, he looked ill. He said the last couple of hours had been very rough and he was feeling under the weather, but he thought everything would be okay.

I thought, *The whole weekend is unraveling and going down the toilet.*

We loaded Mahmoud's luggage into the limo, and we were off. About fifteen minutes from the airport, Mahmoud told me we needed to stop at a drugstore for a couple of items. But those couple of items turned into an hour-and-a-half shopping spree including refilling prescription medications he had forgotten to pack. Luckily, one of my good friends was a cardiologist who had previously treated Mahmoud, so he was able to immediately prescribe the medication.

Now I figured we wouldn't arrive at the hunting lodge until about six o'clock. So much for beating the crowd. About twenty minutes after we left the drugstore and headed toward the hunting lodge, Mahmoud had another problem. He said, "I have a sudden craving for ice cream."

We stopped at a Baskin-Robbins. I assumed we would

go in, Mahmoud would get an ice cream cone to go, and we would leave. But *nooo!* Mahmoud wanted a special sundae, and he wanted to eat it there to avoid getting ice cream on the limo interior. I really didn't give a flying damn about ice cream in the limo because I wanted to get to the lodge. Then Mahmoud got chatty with one of the girls behind the counter. By the time we finally got back on the road, I figured it would be 6:45 p.m. before we got to the lodge.

Then Mahmoud wanted to stop for sunglasses. By that time, I was boiling like a volcano on the inside, thinking of all the things that could possibly be going wrong, but outwardly, I hoped I appeared calm. I said, "You really won't need sunglasses, Mahmoud."

Mahmoud said, "Let's stop anyway."

After fifteen more excruciating minutes, Mahmoud bought his sunglasses and we were on our way again. Without further delays, we finally got to the hunting lodge after seven o'clock.

When we arrived, everyone was there except for Blaien and my outlaw cousin, Phillip Hutchinson, who was helping Blaien with the ducks. It was extremely obvious that some of the guys had started hitting the bottle early. No; they had started *very* early.

After introducing Mahmoud as politely as possible to

everyone, I kept a lookout for Blaien and the ducks, but he was nowhere to be seen. I started to worry. As I worried, we had dinner—steaks, baked potatoes, hot rolls, salad, and dynamite peach cobbler. By then, the booze was really flowing.

At about nine o'clock, Blaien and my cousin Phillip finally rolled in. Blaien told me, "Everything is set. I've got ten live mallards and have put five each in two gunnysacks about thirty yards behind the blind."

I gave him the high five sign and he grinned.

Around 9:30, a group of guys started playing poker, and I joined them. We were playing five-dollar-limit poker because I didn't want someone getting drunk and losing his shirt. When I was a teenager, my parents were afraid I'd become a professional gambler because I played with a group of professionals who came to town each month. We played table stakes or pot limit. At that time, I thought it was normal to come away from a game with $3,000 to $6,000 in cash on me. Today I don't think it's normal for me to carry $1,000 in cash. I probably did gamble more than my share growing up.

Seven of us were playing, and I had an incredible run of cards. By 12:30 a.m. I had probably won 65 percent of the pots. The stack of chips in front of me was larger than the bank. Everyone else was losing.

Suddenly, I heard someone slap someone else on the back. I turned to see Jeff Lewis—who was three sheets to the wind—looking at Mahmoud. He said, "Hey, Mahmoud, what's it going to take for you and me to solve this Arab-Israeli situation?"

I rose up so quickly that the whole poker table lifted a foot off the floor and poker chips bounced off the ceiling in every direction. I sprang over to Jeff and Mahmoud within a millisecond—maybe faster—to remind Jeff about the house rules. "Jeff! No politics are to be discussed this weekend."

Jeff mumbled something incoherently, apologized to Mahmoud, and stumbled over to an armchair.

By that time, I figured we ought to shut it down for the evening and I suggested to the poker players that we void the evening's play. Everyone's money was returned. I didn't get any complaints from anyone.

Ringgg. Ringgg.

Oh boy! Four thirty really does come around early after some serious drinking the night before. By five o'clock, everybody had wobbled into the dining area for coffee. A few people actually ate breakfast, but not many.

It was time to get Mahmoud ready for the hunt. When I went back to the bedroom, I noticed that he had not put on his thermal underwear. I asked him why.

Mahmoud said, "I don't need them."

"You do need them because the temperature is almost freezing with a fifteen-to-twenty-mile-per-hour wind out of the northwest. You'll freeze your rear off if you don't put them on."

So grudgingly, he put them on. After stepping into four pairs of socks, Mahmoud managed to fill the smallest pair waders my employee had picked up. He put on the camouflaged coat and pulled a red deer-hunting cap out of his luggage. He slapped it on his head.

I asked, "What the hell is that?"

Mahmoud replied, "It's a hunting hat. Friends gave it to me in Kuwait, so I'm going to wear it on the hunt."

Trying to keep from laughing, I said, "Mahmoud, we're going duck hunting. All your gear needs to be camouflaged or the birds won't fly close enough for us to shoot them. Most of our shots will be twenty-five to forty yards away. As soon as the ducks see your red hat they will flare and head the other way."

Mahmoud protested but reluctantly exchange his hat for the one we had purchased for him. And then he tucked his red hat into his hunting bag to take along anyway.

We loaded up with a stiff, cold northwest wind blowing from behind. It was pitch black with heavy cloud cover. In fact, you couldn't see a star in the sky. Blaien brought along his Labrador retriever, Bo, and Cousin Phillip had his retriever, Velvet. Blaien would be hunting with Mahmoud and me, my partner Bill, Blaine, and Scooter—who looked to be in really bad shape, one of the major casualties of the night before. Phillip would go with another group.

We drove for about fifteen minutes on shell roads, making three or four turns before Blaien stopped and told us to get out. He said we would need to cross a bar ditch adjacent to the road to get to the wooden walkway out to the blind.

A typical bar ditch has waist-deep water with your waders sinking down into the mud a foot or so. Usually, you've got to strain on each step to get your foot out of the mud. In this area, most bar ditches are ten to twenty feet across.

Blaien crossed first, followed by Scooter.

And then it was Mahmoud's turn. Mahmoud took three steps and his boots sunk into the mud. I went to help. Mahmoud held onto me for leverage and tried to get out, but he couldn't budge. Blaien handed his gun to Scooter and came back for us. So did Bill. It took the three of us real effort in the freezing cold water to finally free Mahmoud. He leaned on Blaien and me for support, and we guided him across the bar ditch. At that point I was already out of breath, and my hands and gloves were totally soaked.

What a way to start the hunt.

After resting for a few minutes, we started walking on the flimsy wooden walkway that extended over the really marshy areas. At its highest point, the bridge was probably six inches above the water, and in some cases, it might have been two to three inches below it. Very seldom was there a handrail, so the going was slow. Blaien carried Mahmoud's gun, and I carried his hunting bag, including his shells.

Splash!

I yelled, "Goddamn!"

Mahmoud had slipped off the wooden walkway and fallen into the marsh. I jumped off to assist him, and within a couple of minutes, we were back onto the wooden walkway, but water had gotten inside Mahmoud's waders. Given the cold weather, I thought the hunt was over.

Mahmoud said, "No. Let's keep going."

We finally made it to the sunken pit blinds where we were going to hunt. So what's a sunken pit blind? Picture a barrel sunk so low into the marsh that when you sat inside it, your head would be about eighteen inches above ground level. This blind had five sunken barrels in a row and a wooden walkway behind them running the full length of the blind. The whole deal was camouflaged with native cane and grasses that sheltered us from the cold, howling wind.

I was on one end of the blind with Mahmoud next to me, then Bill, then Scooter, then Blaien with Bo sitting obediently behind him. Even with all the issues we'd had getting there, we were still about twenty minutes early for shooting time.

I asked Mahmoud, "How are you doing?"

Mahmoud replied, "I don't know about this hunting stuff."

I asked, "Are you cold?"

He replied, "I'm only wet on one side. I think I'll make it."

Ordinarily, duck hunters find that the best shooting time is during the thirty minutes at sunup and thirty minutes at sundown. With great anticipation, about ten minutes before shooting time, we all started to load our shotguns—all of us but Scooter.

Before I could say anything, he stood up and leaned on the front of the blind. The next thing we heard was a horrible cough and a retching sound.

Over the years, I've seen a number of people sick from drinking too much, but I've never heard anything that sounded so god-awful, horribly bad. Everyone was probably thinking, *I sure hope it's not contagious, but if it is, I sure as hell hope I don't catch it.*

Scooter sat down with a thud. About a minute later, he leaned over and started round two, which was worse than the first. About ten minutes into shooting time, Scooter was still at it. I had to feel sorry for him, but still, a humorous thought came into my mind.

I said, "Scooter, every time you lean over, I think the crabs in front of our blind start clicking their claws together in unison. You can almost hear them say, 'Get ready, he's going to do it again.'"

I'm sure Scooter really appreciated that remark!

Hunting in the pit blinds doesn't leave you with any place to move to other than back to the lodge. Luckily, the wind was blowing from behind us, but sitting two feet from vomit probably made a less than desirable trip for my partner and the guide. For those first fifteen minutes of shooting time, with Scooter feeding the crabs, not a duck within the county wanted to come close to our blind.

Ever hopeful, I said, "Mahmoud, just follow my lead. I'll let you know when to shoot." I figured I'd let him have the first shot.

Finally, Scooter finished.

I asked, "Are you okay, Scooter?"

He mumbled something that I took as a *yes*.

About five minutes later, Blaien called a pair of gad-walls, who immediately headed for our decoys. He shouted, "Take 'em, boys!"

We had our heads down, and just as I was getting ready to tell Mahmoud to shoot, when—*Boom! Boom!*

Mahmoud hadn't even gotten the safety off his shotgun before both ducks were in the water. So much for letting Mahmoud have the first shot.

About ten minutes later, a wad of teal buzzed our pond—just out of range—and kept going.

Then Blaien called again as a group of widgeons started to circle. It was classic duck decoying with maybe fifteen ducks setting their wings and heading in. This time, when Blaien said, "Take 'em," everybody except Scooter got up to shoot.

We knocked down six ducks, but Bo had to chase a wounded one to the other side of the pond. I asked Mahmoud how many he had shot.

He replied, "Those ducks fly really fast." He hadn't even fired his gun.

That meant, with only three of us shooting, we had knocked down six ducks—excellent shooting in anybody's book.

As I sat back down in my barrel to watch Bo retrieve

the ducks, I glanced at Scooter. I was horrified by what I saw. Growing up as the son of an orthopedic surgeon, I had spent a lot of time in ERs and operating rooms, both as a visitor and as a patient. I'd seen a number of dead bodies before but I had NEVER seen someone in Scooter's shape. "Death warmed over" doesn't even come close to describing him. His face was ashen and covered with white splotches, and his eyes were closed.

Scariest of all; he was a fantastic duck hunter yet he had not gotten up to shoot.

I yelled, "Scooter, you okay?"

Scooter nodded, opened one eye, and said, "Where am I?"

At that point I knew he was alright.

For the next thirty minutes there was virtually no duck activity. The time had come to give Blaien a previously agreed-upon sign. As I talked to Mahmoud about some of the different grasses in front of the blind, I raised my hands over my head as if I were stretching. Blaien nodded. He got out of the blind and sloshed through the marsh toward a big gunnysack and opened it. As I kept talking to Mahmoud, I occasionally glanced at Blaien to see when he had a duck ready to go. When he had plucked one from the sack, I raised both my hands again as if I were stretching again.

Blaien threw the duck into the air toward the blind. I couldn't believe what I was seeing. The mallard was fatter and bigger than most geese I had ever shot. He was huge. The bird's wings were beating about a hundred million miles per hour as it soared about fifteen feet into the air— and then, *splat!* Into the mud. I couldn't fricking believe it. Blaien had gotten a fricking duck with clipped wings; a procedure used on domestic ducks to keep them from flying off.

I started choking and gasping, thinking my dealings with the Arabs were going up in smoke. Mahmoud asked, "Are you all right?"

I continued to choke and gasp uncontrollably. Blaien turned his hands up, motioning, "What do I do now?"

I continued coughing and turning red. Mahmoud again asked if I was okay.

I nodded that I was. At that point, Mahmoud had not seen any of the drama unfolding behind the blind.

Blaien sloshed through the marsh toward the duck, picked it up, and threw it in the air again, toward the blind.

What the hell?

That bird looked like a B-29 headed straight for the blind. It landed immediately to my left with another huge *splat*. The bird was so close—no more than twelve inches from me—that it actually splashed mud on my face. I started choking and gasping again—I mean really *gasping*—for breath.

Mahmoud must have thought I was having a coronary. He said, "Let's get this man to a hospital!"

Although I was still coughing, and beet red, I waved Mahmoud off, showing I was okay. But he still had no idea what had just happened.

With tears in my eyes, I slowly looked to my left. Holy crap! The devil duck was so close he could peck me on the nose. We continued to eyeball each other nervously, with neither the duck nor I knowing what to do.

If you think you've ever had an uncomfortable moment, it would pale in comparison to me sitting there helplessly trapped. On my right was the undersecretary to the oil minister of Kuwait, and on my left was an attack duck and the sound of a commode swooshing as my future business in the Middle East went down the toilet.

My heart started racing, and I started choking again!

Blaien, who could see how close the duck was, had no idea what to do. So he walked over to the blind, climbed in and asked me, "What do you think about those Houston Oilers?"

It was suddenly like some surreal event out of a Salvador Dali painting. It couldn't be real. But it was! When

Mahmoud started to stand up, I immediately stopped coughing and stood up to block his view of the duck that was contemplating pecking me on the butt. I showed Mahmoud that I was all right, and he sat down. As I stood there for a few moments in stark terror, I wondered if there really was a God. And if there was a God, would he be a merciful God that day? I promised I would amend my wicked ways and be a good person for the rest of my life.

Then I sat down.

The duck was still on my left, eyeballing me, not sure what to make of the situation, and Mahmoud, on my right, was oblivious to everything. For the next five minutes I silently communicated with God, and the duck stayed hidden from my Arab friend.

Suddenly Blaien pointed to the sky. Ducks! He started calling. The ducks circled and came in. There was some shooting, but I don't think I shot my gun. It was just a blur. Two ducks fell, and Bo jumped out of the blind to fetch the first one. I carefully looked to my left.

Yesss! The fricking devil duck that had been tormenting me for the past ten minutes heard the shooting. He must have decided that was not where he wanted to be because he was waddling away. I couldn't believe it. I was fricking saved! For the first time in what seemed like an eternity, my heart started to beat normally.

I was drained. Over the next thirty minutes, we saw a number of duck flocks. At one point, Mahmoud said he needed to take a leak. Without a second thought, I told him to go out behind the blind.

And suddenly, Mahmoud yelled, "Hey, there's a sack of live ducks over here."

Damn! Just when you think you've avoided the dark, black abyss, *WHAM!*

Busted.

In one of the best comebacks I've ever made, I yelled to Mahmoud, "I had the guide put those live ducks over there so we could use them as decoys if it was a slow hunt." Then I turned to Blaien. "Blaien, go put out the live decoys."

Now, if we got caught by the game wardens, we'd be talking jail time. Well, not really; it would be more like fricking Sing Sing.

Blaien released the two gunnysacks of ducks into our pond, and almost immediately, an incredible transformation too place. In twenty years of duck hunting, I had never experienced such activity. It was like every bird in the county suddenly decided they had to land in our pond. Bo didn't even have time to retrieve the downed ducks before we were shooting more. There were ducks everywhere.

Even Scooter finally got up and shot—just once. Then he put his gun down and didn't fire it again.

We were nearing our duck limits when Mahmoud said, "I'm wet and cold. Let's go back to the lodge."

Although there was almost an out-and-out mutiny from Bill, we packed it up and went back to the lodge. We took with us a really nice strap of mixed ducks including gadwalls, widgeon, one green-headed mallard, three green-wing teal, a sprig (pintail), a couple of mottled ducks, a canvasback, and my partner's spooney.

The next morning, I heard the guide's partner took a party to the same blind and they had to shoot all our decoys. Oops.

4

BIG BUCKS

ONE THING YOU quickly learn when you do business with Arabs is that their attitude toward money is a whole lot different than the attitude Americans have toward money. Part of it is the fact that their culture is so different, but another part is the fact that they have so much of it. The more Bill and I dealt with the Arabs, the better we got to know them, and, even though they still frequently surprised us, we grew more comfortable working with them and less surprised by the crazy stuff we saw.

FINANCIAL STATEMENTS

In the early 1980s, we did some real estate deals with a very wealthy Kuwaiti who did not speak fluent English. Consequently, I had communication problems with him from time to time. Most deals that we did were all cash with no financing. A large deal of over three thousand acres was financed by San Jacinto Savings, a major Houston savings and loan at that time with $2 billion in deposits. When we did the deal, my partner and I provided our financial statements to San Jacinto Savings, but our Kuwaiti partner did not. We told Melvin Reist, the president of San Jacinto Savings, that we would provide the Kuwaiti's financial statement at a later date.

So the next time the Kuwaiti was in town, I asked him for his financial statement, and he assured me he would send a copy. About a month later, Melvin Reist called my partner Bill in a panic. The bank examiners were going to be at San Jacinto Savings the following week, and San Jacinto Savings did not have the Kuwaiti's financial statement.

So Bill called the Kuwaiti and said, "Our lender has to have a copy of your financial statement."

The following week the Kuwaiti came to town. Since my partner was tied up with another meeting, I met with the Kuwaiti. He handed me about twenty-eight single-spaced pages that were covered from top to bottom.

"These are my personal assets, and I have no debt. They do not include my corporate holdings."

I looked at the first line of the first page and gagged. The first line read, "Cash and US Government Securities," and the figure was over $563 million! I think that one Kuwaiti personally had more cash on hand than General Motors!

You can be assured Melvin Reist at San Jacinto Savings was a really happy camper with the Kuwaiti's financial statement.

Holy cow, dealing with these Arabs was not unbelievable—it was beyond imagination at times.

SUNDAY BANKING

Money begets money—and it makes banks pay attention. My partner called me one Sunday morning to tell me that Ahmed was in Houston. Ahmed had some friends from the Middle East who were leaving late that afternoon, but they wanted to open some new accounts in a local bank and make deposits before they left.

I told my partner that Ahmed was nuts. All Texas banks and savings and loans were closed because it was Sunday. I suggested that my partner call Melvin Reist, the aforementioned president of San Jacinto Savings, and ask him.

Bill called Melvin at about ten o'clock a.m. and told him about the situation. He asked if there was any way that San Jacinto Savings would please open up on that Sunday to accept the deposits from some of Ahmed's friends. Melvin said he would have to call back.

About half an hour later Melvin called to say that he had made arrangements for two of his employees to go to the San Jacinto Savings main office at noon to open the new accounts.

My partner called me to ask if I would go because he had a conflict: a Houston Oilers football game, for which I had given him my four tickets.

So I said—very sarcastically, "Sure, I don't have anything to do Sunday afternoon, and I would be happy to go hold their hands."

An hour and a half later, I met Melvin at the main office of San Jacinto Savings. There were also two San Jacinto Savings employees there to open the actual accounts. I don't remember exactly how many people Ahmed brought with him, but I think it was three or four. It took about an hour and twenty minutes to get all the paperwork typed up and signed. As I remember, the new deposits amounted to something like $10 million! That was not a small sum during the early 1980s.

Melvin told the Kuwaitis that their money would not be officially deposited until Monday, the next regular business day.

Ahmed and his friends were happy, San Jacinto Savings was happy, and we were happy.

It was the only time I have ever heard of a bank in Texas doing business on a Sunday. As I left, I pulled Melvin aside and told him I owed him one. We made it up to him by inviting him to the next bird-hunting trip that we made in Mexico, and I invited him on one of my duck hunts.

PACKING CASH

In many instances, people actually came to our offices with cash to buy real estate. In one case, a man brought a small suitcase. In another, a man brought a large briefcase. In both instances, the suitcase and the briefcase were filled with hundred-dollar bills. I don't know how much, but I would guess $1 million in the small case and over $2 million in the larger one.

Bill also had similar experiences in dealing with people from the Middle East. He once met a guy who brought *two* suitcases of cash to our office. We told them all that we did not do business with cash. We would be happy to deal with them if their money came directly from a bank, lending institution, or brokerage account via check or wire transfer.

I do need to mention that unlike buying property in the US, in most countries, real estate transactions were commonly made with cash. The seller would sign over the deed, and the deal was done. But we didn't know if the people who came to our office with cash were simply not aware of how real estate sales were consummated in the US, or if the money came from ill-gotten gains such as from drugs or money laundering.

The bottom line: we were not interested. I would not have been surprised if, over a five-year period, we had people bring $20-30 million in cash to our offices.

Our booming reputation with the Arabs definitely presented some unusual situations.

FAMILY INFLUENCE

Bill and I got an even broader impression of Arab wealth when we visited Kuwait. The country was ruled by the royal family, and about fifty merchant families ran the country on a day-today basis. Almost all these families initially made their money by providing goods and services to the royal family. If a prince wanted a purple banana, they would go out, find a purple banana, and charge him for two purple bananas. That's how the merchant families grew in wealth after oil was discovered in Kuwait.

If a company wanted to do major business in Kuwait, the company needed to align itself with one of these significant merchant families. If not, the company would very quickly find out it was virtually impossible to survive profitably without a Kuwaiti sponsor. What most people didn't realize was that these Kuwaiti merchant families were like Fortune 500 conglomerates. Each family was involved in a multitude of businesses, although many specialized in certain industries, like military procurement, electronics, automobiles, construction, and shipping.

The government of Kuwait was and is a major player in the procurement of goods and services in Kuwait, so all these merchant families were dealing daily with the government. At the same time, members of these merchant families were the heads of the governmental agencies that were procuring the goods and services, whether by direct contract or through bids. There were a lot of brother-in-law deals permeating these business transactions. Kickbacks and bribes were a way of life in doing business within the government.

Between many of the Kuwaiti families, there was the mentality of if you scratch my back, I'll scratch yours.

ALGHANIM INDUSTRIES

Alghanim Industries was the largest or second-largest family-owned business in Kuwait. In fact, it was larger than General Motors in the early to mid-1980s. It seemed like Alghanim was involved with everything—travel agencies, automotive, engineering, advertising, consumer credit, insurance, manufacturing, building materials, electronics, consumer goods, transport, home furnishing, talent development, office automation, and the list went on. Today, Alghanim is among the largest privately owned companies in the world.

I met with Ismail Atwan, the executive assistant to the president of Alghanim. We talked about the possibility of Alghanim making a major commitment to building and developing in the US. Ismail said he would speak to the president and see. The president decided to stay closer to home in the Gulf region and the UK for the time being, but individual family members might be interested in looking at US real estate deals on a deal-by-deal basis.

Over the years, I sent Alghanim three deals: one they didn't want to do, another on which they said the timing wasn't right, and the third they said they needed more time on.

When I mentioned to Ahmed that Alghanim was looking at a third deal and taking too long to decide, he said he would do the deal. Ahmed closed on the property thirty days later.

MYSTERY PARTNERS

We learned very quickly that when we did real estate deals with the Kuwaitis, we could never really be sure who all our partners truly were. When we did a deal with Ahmed Al Babtain, we never knew if Ahmed was our only partner or if he had added one or more Al Babtain family members or friends. In a couple of cases, we thought our partners were Ahmed and the government of Kuwait.

You need to be aware that Kuwaiti family units were bound together very tightly and had extremely strong bonds, much stronger than are typically found within US families. Think of the allegiance to a tribe. It was your tribe against everyone else.

In the US, we have separation of church and state. In Kuwait, we did not think there was a separation between the major merchant families that ran the country on a day-to-day basis and the government. They really appeared to be one and the same.

Although Ahmed signed the papers to buy a property, more than likely there were other partners. Given that family members were in positions of power within the government and some of these governmental agencies were investing hundreds of millions of dollars—if not billions— you can see that the lines of ownership could get blurred very easily. The Kuwaitis didn't have the transparency that we have come to expect with most real estate transactions in the US. That was also true with the other Kuwaiti families that we dealt with.

They all had money and were able to close the transactions, but we were never certain who our partners really were.

PERSPECTIVE OF THE ARAB RICH

In early1981, I was talking to a younger Arab from an extremely wealthy family one evening over dinner. I asked him to tell me the story about how he acquired his wealth and what he did with it.

Apparently, when he was twenty-three, he tapped into something like a family trust.

I said, Okay, what does that mean?"

He said in a matter-of-fact tone, "I inherited $100 million."

I was thinking, *This guy is really rich.* "What did you do with that money?" I asked.

He went out and bought a Rolls Royce, a Lamborghini, a Land Rover, a Learjet, a yacht, a very nice home, a chalet in Switzerland, and memberships in some exclusive clubs.

I asked, "What did you do with the rest of the money?"

He replied, "I invested it in the stock market and made

some real estate investments."

I asked, "Well, what have you done with the investments since then?"

"No. No, you don't understand," he said. "That's what I got the first year. I got another $100 million the second year."

I had a difficult time fathoming the information. It was beyond belief. I asked, "What did you do with the money the second year?"

He bought a Suburban, a couple of race cars, some race horses, a bigger jet, another yacht, a home in France, a home in the UK, a vineyard, some antiques and art, and invested the rest in securities and real estate investments.

"What have you done with the investments since then?"

"Ben, you really don't understand. I got another $100 million the third year!"

Absolutely astounding! I thought. "What did you do with *that* money?"

By that time, he had all the boats, planes, cars, houses, and toys one could ever want. So he looked for unusual or unique things to invest in that his buddies didn't have, so he could boast about his investments to his friends.

That was a real eye-opener for me. I was speaking to the eldest son of one of the largest fortunes in Saudi

Arabia, and he was telling it to me like it was; he wasn't holding anything back. It was like I was speaking nonchalantly to my best friend. I was dumbfounded by his casual attitude toward money. Dealing with the Arabs at times was just beyond belief!

ARABS' HOT BUTTON FOR INVESTING

After we had completed a number of real estate deals with the Arabs, I decided to determine what the real hot button was for doing deals with them. I spoke to a few of our clients but wasn't getting anywhere. Then one night, while entertaining an Arab client, I asked what one thing would Arabs want to see in a deal. Was it the structure, the type of real estate, how quickly the money was returned, or the preservation of capital? I was shocked by his response.

He said, "Those things are typically unimportant."

I was shocked!

He continued, "The real important thing is water and pretty pictures."

I said, "I don't understand."

He said, "The whole Arabian Gulf has very little fresh water and few resorts. The real hot button is showing beautiful pictures of properties with lakes, streams, rivers, and resort-type beaches. All the Arabs want those types of properties. It typically does not matter where they are located."

I was completely blown away by his answer.

He continued, "Ben, do you remember going to the barbershop when you were younger and listening to men telling other men about some good real estate deal they had gotten into?"

"Yes."

"Well, think of guys sitting around in a country club with one guy telling everyone else about this great real estate deal he got into and showing them pictures with water. In one instance he's showing his contemporaries the pretty pictures of a property with attractive beaches, lakes, streams, and rivers, and at the same time he is bragging to his buddies that he got into the deal and they didn't."

I was dumbfounded, but what he said was probably true. When you have huge amounts of money and a deal you get into isn't going to change your lifestyle one iota whether it goes up ten times or it goes to zero, then that perspective makes a lot of sense.

We really were dealing with people who fit the same financial profile, and that's how we ended up selling a lot of property to the Arabs.

AHMED'S HOME BY THE LAKE

My partner and I had our offices in Arena Towers I, which was a sister building to Arena Towers II. Both were twenty-story office buildings located on the Southwest Freeway in Houston. We leased the fourteenth floor, which was six floors below the offices of Mel Powers, the builder/owner.

It was a Friday in 1982, and I had one of those butt-ripper days with meetings scheduled in and out of the office all day. I came back to the office about 3:45 p.m. for a meeting at four.

Bill ran into my office and said, "Ben, you've got to go show Ahmed Mel Powers's house right now." Bill had found out that Mel wanted to sell his home in Clear Lake, and he thought Ahmed would love to buy it. As it turned out, Ahmed had flown into Houston the previous night.

I told Bill four things: first, I didn't broker single-family homes. Second, I had never seen the house and didn't know where it was located. Third, I still had four more meetings that afternoon at our offices, and last, rush hour traffic was a nightmare. If we were lucky, it would take two hours in heavy traffic to get from our offices to Clear Lake and almost as much time to come back. I absolutely, under no circumstances wanted to go, and I wasn't planning on going.

Bill said, "You could go in Mel's helicopter."

I asked, "What helicopter?"

"The one parked on top of our building!"

"Are you pulling my leg?"

"No, it's true. Mel uses the helicopter to fly to his house."

I was flabbergasted, but I still didn't want to go.

"Look," Bill began, "I don't have a real estate license, but you do. Take a couple of the secretaries with you as window dressing for Ahmed, and go sell the darn house."

At that point I was starting to waver, but I still had major misgivings and concerns.

"How do you know Mel will let us use his helicopter? When is it available? Does he have a pilot available now? Is there a car for us to use to get us from where the helicopter lands to the house?"

Sure enough, just fifteen minutes later, I was in a helicopter with Ahmed and two of our very attractive secretaries, going somewhere I didn't know to sell a house I'd never seen.

As we got closer to the house, I asked the pilot, "How long is the car ride from where we land to the house?"

He replied, "You'll see."

The next thing I knew, we were landing at Mel's house in the high-end subdivision of Nassau Bay where most of the astronauts lived. In a heliport! Leapin' lizards, the house had its own heliport!

We got out, and I was still pissed about having to babysit Ahmed. We walked down to the home's dock on Clear Lake, which empties into Galveston Bay. I said to Ahmed, "There's the dock."

Well, this was no ordinary dock. You could probably have berthed a destroyer along it. I notice the swimming pool to my left and told Ahmed, "There's the pool." I didn't even know the house had a pool.

I went to the back door, unlocked the house, and told Ahmed, "Here's the house," without going inside. Ahmed went inside with our two secretaries, whose eyes were as big as dinner plates. About five minutes later Ahmed came back out. He said, "There is a problem."

I asked, "What kind of problem?"

"I would like to buy the house, but I want to buy it with all the furniture and paintings included."

"Really?"

"Yes. I want everything in the house except clothes and personal items."

Astonishing!

An hour later, I had a contract signed by both Mel Powers and Ahmed for a house I'd never seen before that afternoon. It was surreal. A month later, Ahmed closed on the house for a little less than $1.3 million—all cash, no financing.

Never in my life have I ever brokered a property so easily, and I have brokered over a billion dollars in real estate throughout the years.

ARENA TOWERS

The total net rentable office space in the two Arena Towers buildings was about 875,000 square feet.

Ahmed came up to our offices one day and out of the blue asked, "Are the two Arena Tower buildings available for sale?"

Bill told him we didn't know, but that we could find out very quickly since the owner officed six floors above us. He called Mel Powers and asked if he would consider selling the Arena Towers.

Mel Powers said, "Make me an offer."

An hour later I handed Mel Powers a $100 million offer to buy both buildings for cash!

The negotiations went back and forth for a couple of weeks, with Ahmed raising his offer to $110 million, but in the end, Mel Powers decided to keep the buildings. Later we found out that he had a personal penthouse on top of one of the buildings that he didn't want to give up.

In retrospect, I'm sure Mel regretted not selling the

Arena Towers to Ahmed until the day he died because eventually the buildings went down in value. Ultimately, they were foreclosed on by a lender in one of Houston's down markets.

That would not have been a problem for Ahmed because he planned to pay cash out of pocket for both buildings.

Just another typical day at the office.

SOUK AL-MANAKH

In August of 1982, the Souk al-Manakh—Kuwait's stock market— crashed. It was the largest stock market crash of all time with losses estimated at a staggering $94 billion.

How did it happen?

In the 1970s, the price of oil increased dramatically which led to incredible stock price appreciation in the Kuwait stock market. As the price of oil went up, more money was available for investments, leading to what appeared to be an endless appreciation of the Kuwaiti stocks.

Only sheiks could grant new corporate business charters, and only corporations could trade stock publicly. The royal family of Kuwait granted very few new charters because they did not want to fuel more speculation.

That resulted in a shortage of available stocks to trade in Kuwait.

That, in turn, led to a new over-the-counter stock market called the Souk al-Manakh. The market was housed in an air-conditioned parking garage that at one time had been a camel-trading market. The market specialized in highly speculative and nonregulated stocks from Arab countries that were non-Kuwaiti. At its peak, the capitalization of the Souk al-Manakh was the third highest in the world, behind only the US and Japan. It was larger than the individual capitalization of the UK, German, or French stock exchanges. It was truly unbelievable!

The Souk al-Manakh became the largest speculative market in the world. People bought stocks on 100 percent margin, paying with postdated checks that were for more money than the current price because they included interest. In turn, that created explosive growth and huge, unregulated credit expansion. At the height of the speculation, interest rates reached 100 percent!

In August 1982, it all came tumbling down. It really didn't crash; it just stopped because there were no buyers. It was triggered by a stock dealer who presented a postdated check for payment on the day it was due, and the check bounced. At that time, the speculation was just utter fantasy. The worst offender had financed $14 billion worth of stock purchases with $14 billion in debt. Two years previously, the same person had been a passport clerk!

In September of 1982, the Kuwait Finance Ministry ordered all Souk al-Manakh checks to be turned in for clearance, and the exchange was officially closed. The official government accounting of the losses was a staggering $94 billion from approximately six thousand speculators—an average loss of over $15 million per investor.

The bursting of that speculative bubble had major repercussions throughout the whole Gulf region, and it was one of the major causes for a recession. All the banks but one, the National Bank of Kuwait, were technically insolvent. In fact, the National Bank of Kuwait was the only Kuwaiti bank to survive the crisis intact. Subsequently, the government started implementing new financial regulations to prevent similar occurrences in the future. These regulations were continuing when Iraq invaded Kuwait and everything changed.

Another important but unpublicized event occurred that had serious negative consequences to our Arab partners and to us. The emir, the Kuwaiti king, called in the heads of all the major Kuwaiti families and told them there was a major financial crisis because of the Souk al-Manakh. These families were told that they had to show solidarity with Kuwait by not moving any funds out of the country until the crisis passed. It meant that, even though most of our clients did not participate in the Souk al-Manakh and had extremely good cash positions, they could not transfer funds overseas to make payments on existing obligations—like land purchases.

Although many of the purchases made by the Arabs in Houston were for cash, some were financed. Even though they had cash in the bank, the Kuwaitis could not meet the due principal-and-interest payments. As a result, we lost a number of deals because our partners were unable to make the total principal-and-interest payments.

A MAJOR LOSS

One of the lost deals lost to Souk al-Manakh really burned. My partner and I had sought a large land tract for a long-term residential subdivision development in the Houston area. About thirty-five miles north of Houston, I found a thirty-seven-hundred-acre wooded tract—over six square miles of land—owned by Champion Paper. The tract looked like a perfect fit for what we wanted to do, except there were numerous pipelines and an overhead primary electrical transmission line.

After going over the tract preliminarily with Larry Milberger, our engineer with R.G. Miller Engineers, we decided to go ahead and buy the tract with Ahmed Al Babtain as our partner. I don't remember the exact price, but I think it was around $4,750 per acre for a total of approximately $17.5 million.

A major obstacle came up in the negotiations. At the last minute, Ahmed decided it would be nice if a friend of his—who was a broker and will remain nameless—got a fee. We are talking about giving up over half a million in a consulting fee to someone who, among other things, was supposedly deported from the UK! My partner agreed to Ahmed's request, although I was not happy. It was the right thing to do for the long run in dealing with the Arabs, but I thought it was complete lunacy.

We paid 20 percent down at closing—$3.5 million—with a ten-year note having principal and interest payable annually. Immediately, we started land planning the development. We decided that the best way to hide the pipelines was to set up a number of interconnecting lakes with five eighteen-hole golf courses that would be overseen by one country club. We imagined a place that would appeal to someone who wanted to get out of town for the weekend without having to be on the road for two to three hours to get there. In addition, creating all the lakes and golf courses would make it a destination resort that was easily assessable to Houstonians.

As the plan evolved over the next year, we started creating six water districts to provide water and sanitary sewer and an overall Water and Improvement District (WCID) to coordinate drainage. The property was so flat that we needed major water detention onsite and major offsite drainage. We made a principal-and-interest payment of approximately $2.8 million at the end of the first year.

Every time we turned around, it seemed the plan morphed into a larger development. I'm sure our engineers loved it. The ultimate plan would require us to move three million cubic yards of dirt, which would have been the largest earth-moving job in Texas history at that time.

Just as we were getting ready to start actual project development in August of 1982, the Souk al-Manakh collapsed. The bottom line: we lost the property in foreclosure to Champion Paper after we had paid them approximately $6.8 million in cash. We were absolutely sick.

Such were the perils of dealing with the Kuwaitis and the Souk al-Manakh.

A SHIPLOAD OF VOLVOS

Our Arab friends were interested in more than doing just real estate deals with us. One day Ahmed came to the office and met with Bill and me. Again, Ahmed had a problem. He was selling a shipload of six hundred Volvos to someone in Saudi Arabia who had changed his mind at the last minute.

When I say at the last minute, the ship had already sailed from Sweden and was scheduled to arrive in Saudi Arabia in two days.

Ahmed asked if my partner and I wanted to buy the Volvos at cost. It would only be $9.6 million!

I was thinking, *Only $9.6 million cash at a point in time we barely have two nickels to rub together,* but of course, we told Ahmed we were interested.

After Ahmed left, I said, "Where are we going to get $9.6 million with one hundred percent financing? We don't even have the money for a down payment."

We kicked around various ideas and finally decided to go talk to our banker. We explained to him that we were broke—which he already knew—but told him we could buy six hundred brand-new Volvos for $9.6 million, which was Ahmed's cost.

He asked, "Do you have a manifest?"

My partner and I exchanged blank stares and said, "No."

"Well, the first thing you need to do is get me a copy of the manifest, and we'll consider a loan."

After our meeting, we immediately called Ahmed,

and he faxed a copy of the manifest directly to our banker. The next day our banker called and said the bank would loan us $10.2 million to buy the Volvos. We were in shock. Not only was the bank loaning us 100 percent of the money to buy the Volvos, but they were also loaning us a six-month interest reserve. Unbelievable!

We thought the Volvos might be saleable quickly for $24,000 each. We called Ahmed and told him we thought we could put the deal together and asked him to fax over a copy of the manifest. We made two copies, and each of us started going through the list of cars.

Cars.

Wrong!

One-third of the vehicles were large trucks that were marketable for more than individual cars.

The next day our banker and my partner had lunch, and our banker casually mentioned that our price to purchase the Volvos was substantially below the wholesale cost.

My partner asked, "How could that be?"

Our banker told him, "Ahmed buys in such large volume yearly that he probably has the cheapest dealer price in the world."

Absolutely incredible!

We were now pumped more than ever about the deal

and were picking out specific Volvos for our families, friends, and employees. Everything rocked along for five days until I had lunch with a friend. During lunch, I excitedly told him about our deal to buy six hundred Volvos and asked if he wanted to buy one.

He responded, "Is the steering column on the left or right side?"

"Duh . . . I don't know." As panic crept into my brain, I told my friend that I had to go. I immediately called my partner and asked him, "Are the steering columns on the right side or left side?"

The answer was, "Duh . . . I don't know."

We were two peas in a pod. Bill immediately called Ahmed and asked, "Are the steering columns on the left or right side?"

Ahmed immediately replied, "On the right side, of course."

Bill was stunned but didn't tell Ahmed that we might have a huge problem. He immediately called me and in a panicky voice said, "They are on the right. What do we do now?"

I said, "You know you can refit the steering columns and move them from the right to the left, but I don't know how much it will cost." We both promptly started making calls to find someone knowledgeable about refitting the vehicles. After half an hour or so, we found someone who quoted us a price of $4,550 per vehicle. He asked us to forward a copy of the manifest to him.

If the cars cost $16,000, $4,550 to repair, $800 for brokerage, and $650 for legal and interest carry, we would still make $2,000 per car. That's still a $1.2 million profit. We were saved!

Or so we thought.

About fifteen minutes later we got a call back from the guy who had just quoted us $4,550 per car to fix the problem. He said, "You didn't tell me that about a third of the vehicles are large trucks."

I asked, "Does that matter?"

"Well, the trucks are a lot more complicated and will cost $15,700 each to retrofit."

"That doesn't work. Are there any alternatives?"

"Sell them in a country where you don't have to refit the steering columns, or don't buy the Volvos."

"We'll get back to you."

Damn! Double damn! Things were starting to look bleak. To retrofit all the cars and trucks would cause us to lose over a million dollars.

I explained the situation to my partner, and his response was, "We are undeniably in the toilet. How do we get out?"

Our only hope was to find someone to buy six hundred Volvos in Europe, Africa, or South America that Ahmed hadn't already spoken to. So we both got on the phone and started calling people we knew who had overseas connections to see if they could help.

The next day a contact whom we'll call Pedro called. He said, "I think I can make the deal work."

Bill said, "Great, but it's got to be quick."

Pedro said, "I think I can get General Noriega in Panama to buy the Volvos. One of his top advisors told me that he thought they could immediately sell all the trucks to the Bolivian army. They'll buy them for twenty-three thousand dollars each, and you'll pay me a thousand-dollar finder's fee per vehicle. They can close next Friday."

I looked at Bill, who was already nodding yes.

I said, "Pedro, draw up the deal and we'll sign it. Send a faxed copy to our attorneys and to us."

Pedro said his attorney would draw it up, and we'd have a draft that afternoon.

The draft came that afternoon, and it looked good. We called our attorney, Michael O'Brien, who said it was a very simple, straightforward agreement, but he might suggest a couple of changes.

I said, "If it's not crucial, we don't want to make any changes. We want this deal closed yesterday!"

"Sign it."

We signed a copy and faxed it back to Pedro.

The next day we had a signed contract from Noriega. Unbelievable! If everything went as it was supposed to, the deal would go down as follows:

Sales price of the 600 Volvos	$13,800,000
Cost of 600 Volvos	$9,600,000
Finder's fee	$600,000
1.5% financing fee	$144,000
Legal and closing costs	$50,000
Profit	**$3,406,000**

We faxed Ahmed a contract to buy the Volvos for $9.6 million and that said we wanted the Volvos delivered to Panama City, Panama.

That same day, Ahmed faxed back a signed contract, but he had made a change. He wanted an additional $250,000 for shipping.

We signed the deal. Okay, we're still making over $3 million!

For the next nine days, we held our breath and waited. Based on our previous experiences in smaller deals, we knew there were always concerns such as the buyer not closing, delays, and last-minute, unexpected changes or fees.

The day before the closing, the news came. Noriega

wanted us to pay an additional fee of $1.8 million as a brokerage commission to someone we had never heard of! You've got to be kidding me.

We called Pedro and told him we were not willing to pay an additional $1.8 million fee at closing to some broker we didn't know even existed.

Pedro told us that the broker was the one who had negotiated the deal for the sale of the trucks to the Bolivian army. If we didn't pay the fee, it could blow the deal. We told Pedro we'd call him back.

Five minutes later—after my partner and I stopped cursing—we called Pedro back.

I said, "Pedro, we are not happy, but if this guy really did broker the trucks, he should get something, but not $1.8 million. Try to get a more reasonable price for the commission."

Over the next six hours there were numerous telephone calls, faxes, and curse words. In the end, we agreed to pay $1.1 million. The next day we had one of the smoothest closings we have ever had.

After the closing had been completed, we asked Pedro, "How much did Noriega sell the Volvo trucks for?"

Pedro said, "Fifty thousand dollars apiece!"

I quickly did the math. "You mean he ended up buying four hundred Volvos from us for $3,735 each after the sale to the Bolivians?"

Pedro said, "That's right, except we don't know if Noriega got a portion or all of the $1.1 million commission. If he got all of it, the actual cost would be more like $985 each."

Unbelievable! We probably left a bunch of money on the table at closing, but as they say, "Easy come, easy go." We still ended up making over $2 million. We were in the berries!

Gadzooks!

Another day in the life of dealing with the Arabs. They always had bright ideas for making big money.

LIGHTBULBS

On one of his trips to Houston, Mahmoud said he had a bright idea for making a lot of money.

"What is it?" I asked.

"Lightbulbs."

"You want to sell the Kuwait government lightbulbs?"

"Yes, but not any old incandescent lightbulb." He wanted to sell the government of Kuwait lightbulbs that lasted five years. "Do you realize how much money the government would save on changing lightbulbs? If the government wanted lightbulbs to remain on twenty-four hours a day where there was a very high ceiling and a ladder was required to change lightbulbs, the savings would be huge."

I said, "That's great! Where are you going to get these lightbulbs?"

Mahmoud said, "That is your job." He came up with the idea, and he expected me to find a source.

I said, "I'm not a lightbulb expert, but I'll definitely check around."

The next day I started calling retail lightbulb sources and then manufacturers. The result was that Mahmoud had a great idea, but he was ahead of the times. Back then, I could not find any manufacturer making lightbulbs that lasted for five years.

It's too bad the technology we have today wasn't available thirty years ago. It could have been a very profitable venture.

BAHRAIN

As you can imagine, word got out about the deals we were doing in the Middle East, and by the mid 80s, we were getting a number of off-the-wall proposals from people around the world who wanted our help to do business in the Middle East.

One of the more unusual proposals came around late 1984 or early 1985. A gentleman came to my office and said he was interested in dealing with the government of Bahrain. Bahrain was an island off the east coast of Saudi Arabia and southeast of Kuwait.

He said, "The government wishes to improve the soil in Bahrain and make the country a garden-spot destination resort for the whole Middle East."

Bahrain allowed alcohol service, something other Middle Eastern countries did not—at least not legally or in public. If they could beautify the country by converting the desert into a lush, blooming paradise, Bahrain would become the destination of choice for Middle Eastern getaways.

The gentleman said he wanted to make a proposal. He had worked out a plan to import enough manure to cover the whole island a foot deep. Mixing the manure with the naturally-occurring sand and covering it with topsoil would allow virtually anything to grow there.

I told him I only saw four problems with his idea.

The first was the lack of fresh water. Where was Bahrain going to get the fresh water to grow the plants? Second, temperatures get very hot in the Middle East and would cause most plants and trees to burn up even if they had adequate water. Third, sandstorms. They would blow the topsoil away or bury the plants in sand. Fourth, and most importantly, was the stench that would be created by dumping a foot of manure on the whole island.

He said, "I'll get back to you."

You know, I never heard from him again. But I did hear from other people wanting to get involved with the Kuwaitis through me.

GULF OIL CORPORATION DEAL

After my partner got off the phone with a well-known Texas oilman, he came into my office and said, "You fricking won't believe who just called me."

I had no idea.

He said, "T. Boone Pickens."

"The corporate raider?"

"Yes."

I asked, "Why is he calling you?"

"He wants to make a hostile-takeover offer for Gulf Oil Corporation," he said. "He wants us to approach the Kuwait Oil Ministry to see if they would be interested in being his financial partner. So I'm asking you, would you please call Mahmoud Al Adasani to have him speak to the oil minister or emir and see if the government of Kuwait would be interested in being T. Boone Pickens's financial backer on this deal?"

I told my partner it was extremely unlikely that the Kuwaiti government would want to get involved in any hostile-takeover bid. If Gulf Oil Corporation agreed to be taken over by a T. Boone Pickens entity, I thought the Kuwait government would be extremely interested in providing all or most of the funding. I told him the reason was that the Kuwaitis typically were not interested in getting into any type of adversarial relationship. They wanted to be friendly with everybody because they didn't want to rock the boat. A hostile takeover of a major oil company went against the way Kuwaitis normally did business. Yes, they wanted to make money, but they were not interested in creating conflict. They were more interested in preservation of capital and keeping good working relations with as many people as possible, as opposed to making more money.

I concluded, "But I'll call the undersecretary and ask."

Then I called Mahmoud and explain the deal to him. He told me, almost verbatim, what I had already told my partner. He said he would check with the oil minister and emir and get back to me, but he did not think the government of Kuwait would be interested.

A few days later Mahmoud called to say the Kuwait government would not be interested in getting involved with a hostile takeover, but if Gulf Oil Corporation was interested in being taken over in a mutually agreeable, friendly takeover, then the government of Kuwait would like to sit down and discuss financing the deal further.

Gulf Oil wasn't interested in being taken over. T. Boone Pickens found other financial backers and made a hostile-takeover bid. I think that resulted in the Gulf Oil Corporation paying off the raider, and they went away.

5

IRAQ TRIP: ABANDONED!

S O AS YOU have probably guessed by reading all of my stories about working with Arabs, by the time the Iraqi modular home inspiration occurred to me, I was reasonably comfortable with the idea of doing business with Arabs I had not yet met.

Three days after Mahmoud gave the thumbs up for the modular home concept, I found myself flying to Kuwait higher than a kite, thinking my post-war reconstruction venture had to be a home run. If we could capture 25 percent of the market, we could very well generate half a billion dollars in sales over a three-year period. Because the Iraqi government was receiving US aid for reconstruction of the country, and Mahmoud had strong political contacts because of his former position, I envisioned returning to Houston with signed contracts in hand.

After I checked into the Meridian Hotel in Kuwait

City, I called Mahmoud.

He said, "Everything is set for us to go to Basra tomorrow morning on a bus. I'll pick you up at six thirty at the entrance to the hotel."

Six-thirty? In the morning? Mahmoud once told me he wasn't an early riser, and he'd proven that each time he stayed with me in Houston. The timing seemed odd.

I could hardly sleep that night because I was so keyed up. What if we got 50 percent of the business? Even better: what if Mahmoud could negotiate an exclusive contract for us to provide *all* the new homes? It could represent billions in sales.

I had a lot of questions about real estate in Basra, but no answers. Were their building sites scattered here and there throughout the city, or were whole subdivisions available? What size homes were currently on the market? What kind of exterior building materials did they use? And what about access? I wanted to know what types of roads they had and whether those roads could handle heavy loads. Any adjacent negatives were important to be aware of, such as rail yards, refineries, dump sites, dilapidated buildings, and so on. And what about adjacent farmland or undeveloped acreages? Could any schools and shopping areas be found? What type of utilities did they have? Was the terrain level, hilly or mountainous?

Questions whirred throughout the night.

The next morning Mahmoud picked me up as planned and we headed to the bus station.

As he parked his Mercedes, he said, "There's been a change in plans. I'm not going with you."

He wasn't coming with me? A red flag instantly went up.

"But don't worry," Mahmoud continued. "I've arranged for an English-speaking limo driver to take you to view potential building sites around Basra and then return you to Kuwait."

I asked, "Why aren't you going?"

He replied calmly, "I just don't want to go."

Now red flags started waving. *Are you kidding me?* I thought. I asked Mahmoud, "Have you ever been to Iraq?"

"Well, no," he said. "And I don't think the time is right for me to go now."

He didn't seem alarmed or upset, but he just wasn't going. Period. At that time, I had no idea why he had changed his mind, but an ominous feeling came over me. I didn't speak Arabic. I was going to a country I'd never been to before. Many Iraqis hated Americans. I am Jewish. And I was going *alone*. What could possibly go wrong?

Mahmoud walked into the bus station with me. He handed me my ticket and the contact information for my English-speaking limo driver in Basra, and said, "Good luck."

I said, "Thanks." But I was thinking, *What the hell have I gotten myself into?*

As I walked to the bus, I couldn't believe my eyes. It was the most beautiful bus I had ever seen in my life! I mean *ever*! It was black with silver swirls and what looked like walnut wood trim that was surely metal. The inside of the bus was even nicer. There were two plush leather seats on either side of a very wide aisle covered in thick carpeting. The seats folded back like big Lazy Boy recliners, and there were headphones so you could listen to the radio. There wasn't a rock star in the universe who wouldn't have killed to own this bus. It was absolutely beautiful and beyond my wildest dreams for a bus.

It was that good.

Well, maybe Mahmoud was right; I wouldn't have any problems.

The bus was half-full when we pulled out of the station. It rode like a dream and was incredibly quiet. As we drove, some of my anxiety began to dissipate. The bus was supposedly taking me directly to the hotel in Basra where, I presumed, I would meet my English-speaking limo driver.

Easy peasy, right?

But a nagging question echoed in my mind: *What could possibly go wrong? What could possibly go wrong?*

About thirty-five minutes later, in the middle of the desert, the bus pulled into what must have been a parking lot of compacted sand. A plain metal building, roughly ten thousand square feet, sat in the middle. The area was absolutely desolate without a tree or shrub in sight. Although thirty or forty cars might have fit on the lot, it was empty too.

When the bus stopped, the passengers started getting out. My stomach tightened and my butt cheeks clenched. I held back until I was the last person on the bus. I went up to the driver and asked, "What's happening?"

"We're at the Kuwaiti border, and you have to go through Kuwaiti customs before you can leave the country."

"Oh," I said, relieved. That was a normal procedure. I had gone through customs at airports before, which was no big deal. I got off the bus and my hindquarters started to unclench.

Starting to feel a lot better, I joked with some of the Kuwaiti agents as I went through customs. But when I went outside after my passport was finally stamped, I looked around the parking lot and there was no fricking bus! A group of thirty to thirty-five people gathered in an area about fifty feet away, so I joined them. Five minutes passed. Then ten minutes. Then twenty minutes. Still no bus. Although we were standing in the shade, it was summer in Kuwait, and it was already starting to get really hot.

Then a battered yellow school bus with Arabic writing on the front and chicken coops tied down on top turned into the parking lot. Big clouds of sand billowed behind—right out of *The Beverly Hillbillies*. The bus came to a screeching halt in front of us, with the sand cloud engulfing the entire group. Everyone instantly started hacking and coughing.

The bus door opened, and people began to board. All of a sudden, I was the only one left standing outside the bus. I had no earthly idea where this thing was going, but reluctantly, I boarded. The bus was so crowded that I had to stand on the first step inside the door. Once again, my butt cheeks tightened a little. The bus was not air-conditioned and probably had thirty people over its suggested maximum capacity. It was hot as hell inside.

For the next fifteen minutes, the bus travelled through no-man's-land for two to three hundred feet, stopped, then made a ninety-degree turn, went another two to three hundred feet, stopped, and made another nine-ty-degree turn. Then the bus stopped and the doors flew open—much to the relief of my butt cheeks.

A dusty sign just outside announced: "Iraq."

You know all those stories you read in the newspapers about Iraqis hating Americans? It was absolutely true at that customs station! Since I had been the last person to board the bus, I was the first person off and the first person to go through customs clutching my American passport.

A custom agent bellowed at me in a voice so loud that heads turned. "You. American. Come here!" As he hauled me aside, everyone else lined up and other custom agents were stamping their documents right and left. My fellow bus passengers streamed through customs and out the door.

The agent with me went through all of my paperwork three times. He barked, "Stay here," and he left the room. Five to ten minutes later, he returned with another man—maybe a supervisor—and I went through the whole pro-cess again. When the second man was finished looking at my paperwork, he told me to have a seat. He and the first agent marched off to speak with a group of five or six additional people. From my vantage point, it looked like they were arguing about what to do with me.

Finally, the first guy returned, stamped my documents, and pointed towards the exit. Relieved that I was finally done with that process, I skipped out the door—fifteen minutes after everyone else had gone through.

I stepped into the bright Iraqi sunshine and—aw fudge nuggets—there was no bus again. But this time there was no group of people either. They were all gone! What now? I didn't speak Arabic, and I was in Iraq where I knew no one, the Iraqis I'd met so far really seemed to hate Americans, and I had no idea how to get to Basra.

It's going to be okay, it's going to be okay. I've at least made it to Iraq! I kept telling myself that, but holy mackerel, I was feeling something completely different than okay.

Finally, I spied five guys huddled together about a block away. Thinking they might be cab drivers, I walked over to the first one and asked, "Basra?"

He nodded.

"How much?"

He gave me a blank stare.

I asked again, "How much?"

Another blank stare.

I pulled out my wallet and asked, "How much?"

In a heavily accented voice, he said, "One hundred dinars."

That was about $340. No way! I didn't just fall off the turnip truck. I opened my wallet, pulled out three American twenty-dollar bills, and handed them to him. He looked at them, threw them on the ground, stomped on the money, and all the men walked off in a huff!

My backside didn't stay relaxed for long. (Okay, I might have a minor problem here!)

I was hot, sweaty, and agitated. It was time for Plan B, which I hadn't even begun to figure out. I spotted a long adobe wall stretching into the distance. About a block away from me, a large tree grew behind the wall, maybe an oak. One of its limbs hung over the street side, providing some shade.

I stooped down, picked up my money, walked over to the shaded area, and sat down to regroup.

What the hell am I going to do now? I wondered. In a normal world worst-case scenario, I would have called a cab to take me to Basra. Unfortunately, it wasn't a normal world for me. I probably couldn't find a phone I could use, and if I did, I couldn't order a cab because I didn't speak Arabic. Most of the people I'd dealt with before in the Middle East spoke terrific English, but so far, any English I'd heard from Iraqis was limited and All I could think was, *It's going to be okay, it's going to be okay!*

About five minutes later, a kid who looked about ten

or eleven years old rode up on an old, battered bicycle. He was wearing torn, baggy pants and a shirt that looked two sizes too big. He stopped, and in broken English asked, "What is wrong?"

I said, "I want to go to Basra."

He motioned for me to follow him.

What the hell. How much worse could it get? So I got up and started to follow the kid. We went to the end of the wall and turned down a dusty street—I'm being kind; it was more like a dirt trail—walked another block, and then turned into what looked to be a group of old two-story, flat-roof tenement buildings from the 1950s. We walked by rows of outdoor clotheslines on which clothes hung over bumpy streams of green, brown, and purple sewage.

Although there was little noticeable aroma, I had misgivings about wearing clothes that had dried all day over open sewage. It didn't seem very appealing to me, but what the hey, I was just a visitor to their country who was absolutely lost. We made a couple more turns. By then, I had no idea how to find my way back to the adobe wall where he had found me in the first place.

We then entered a pretty little square, and on the other side of the square sat a twenty-passenger bus.

The boy pointed to the bus and said, "Basra."

I tried to tip the boy, but he wouldn't take any money. Under the circumstances, I thought it strange that a poor boy wouldn't accept any money for helping me out. Maybe his parents had taught him to never take anything from a stranger—particularly an American stranger. I thanked him and turned to the bus.

A man I assumed to be the driver stood next to the bus door as if he was waiting for passengers.

I approached him and said, "Basra?"

He nodded.

"How much?"

"One Kuwaiti dinar."

That equaled about $3.40. I paid him, got on the bus as his first passenger, and sat down on the back seat.

I'm saved, I thought.

The first guy who got on after me carried a rifle and bandolier but wore no uniform. That was not a very reassuring sight to see. As if I hadn't already had some major misgivings about my whole cockamamie trip to Iraq. I now had what appeared to be an armed guard on the bus. Maybe each bus in the area travelled with an armed guard to protect the passengers from bandits or terrorists.

That wasn't such a bad idea, but the next two men to enter the bus were also armed; one had *two* rifles! Either I had three armed guards on the bus or two of the guards had mistakenly gotten on the wrong bus.

I started to feel a little queasy. Geez Louise, what else could go wrong?

Then a group of six men got on the bus.

Yeah, you guessed it. They were all armed to the teeth, and nobody wore a uniform.

When the bus left to go to Basra, there were eighteen people on the bus, plus the bus driver, but I was the only one who wasn't armed. Even the bus driver had a large pistol jammed in his belt in front of his belly. I should have asked one of the guys with two weapons if I could borrow one of his!

What could possibly go wrong in a situation like this?

I began to think that in the best-case scenario, I'd been captured to be held for ransom. It wasn't a very appealing option, but it was sure as hell better than any of the other options I thought of at the time. They could be planning to have their way with me sexually, make movies of me saying anti-American slogans, use me for forced labor as a slave, torture me, or kill me.

As my mind spun, my heart raced. When you start thinking that the best option available to you is for your captives to kill you quickly, you have a problem. All I could think about was self-preservation, and in a bus full of potential bandits and kidnappers, that did not seem likely.

I have always been an above average problem solver. When I have a problem, I keep turning over the options, even when I go to sleep. Suddenly, I wake up at, let's say three in the morning, and I'll have a solution to the problem. But that trip? Well, I went on that trip knowing there'd be a few bumps in the road, but I didn't expect to be riding down that road in a dump truck from hell.

I sank into my bus seat drenched with sweat, and I don't think it was only because of the heat. Although I had lost a lot of liquid through perspiration, I didn't feel thirsty. I was in utter disbelief about everything that was happening to me and just a tad distressed. All those years bumbling along with the Arabs, and it never occurred to me that Iraq could be so different from Kuwait.

6

KUWAIT SOCIETY AND CUSTOMS

MOST PEOPLE THINK of Kuwait as being hot and dry. In fact, it may have the hottest average temperature of any country in the world. What most people don't realize is that Kuwait is normally extremely humid because it is located on the Arabian Gulf.

I do not believe that Kuwait has any natural fresh water. They did have the two largest desalination plants in the world, and when I travelled to Kuwait in the 1980s, those plants provided fresh water for a population of over two million people.

Of those two million people, less than 30 percent were Kuwaiti citizens, and the bulk of the balance was made up of Palestinians who were the workers. To be a Kuwaiti citizen meant that you were privileged. You got free milk and cheese every month from the government. You received free health care for life and free education from elementary school to college. Kuwaiti families also received a social allowance of $275 per month, per child, until the child reached his or her eighteenth birthday. That was not welfare; it was paid to every family regardless of income. When a Kuwaiti got married, he received a $12,000 payment from the government plus a free house. In the 1980s the cheapest homes were going for $200,000 or more. Not bad for just being born in Kuwait.

Of the Kuwaiti citizens, there were five to six thousand real players scattered among forty or fifty Kuwaiti families. These were the decision makers, the people who controlled most of the wealth in Kuwait, and happened to be the people we dealt with. They provided the goods and services to the royal family.

Kuwait is very different from the US in many respects, from their legal system and the way they treat women to their attitudes toward food, money, and cars. Spending time there was a real eye-opener.

A TOUGH LEGAL SYSTEM

I don't know if this is correct, but on my first trip to Kuwait in 1982, I was led to believe the following by a Kuwaiti attorney: the legal system was weighed heavily toward convictions in criminal matters. Justice was swift and severe. Appeals happened very quickly—I think within thirty days of the end of a trial—and they usually resulted in the affirmation of the original conviction. You didn't want to do anything in Kuwait that could possibly land you in their legal system as a defendant in a criminal case.

To put this in context, in 1984, I believe there were only two murders in the whole country of Kuwait with its population over two million people, and foreigners committed both murders! I think it lends credence to what I was told about the legal system.

Messing with the law in Kuwait was a stupendously stupid idea.

PALESTINIANS IN KUWAIT

In the mid-1980s there was a major push to possibly expel all Palestinians from Kuwait—despite the fact that they formed the bulk of workers in Kuwait. That would have created unbelievable problems for the Kuwaitis because they were not prepared to do menial tasks. If not the Palestinians, then another source of cheap labor would have to be imported. Samia (Sami) Amarneh was a Palestinian who ran the day-to-day operations for the Adasani's plastic pipes and fittings factory. Yousif Al Adasani was the general manager. While I was on a tour of the plant, I met Sami. She said she wanted to speak to me after I finished looking at the plant.

After the tour was over, I went into Sami's office, where she told me the Adasanis had always said nice things about me, and that I was an unusually good problem-solver. Sami told me she and her husband, Jihod, had a problem and needed help, and they wanted to invite me over for dinner so we could discuss the problem further. I agreed to meet for dinner, so she gave me her address and suggested seven o'clock.

Sami and her husband lived in an area that was nice but not expensive for Kuwait; all areas of Kuwait were expensive compared to Houston. She introduced me to Jihod, who worked for the Kuwait Institute for Scientific Research as a scientist doing work in electronics and automation engineering.

Over drinks Sami explained the problem she and her husband faced. Politicians had been debating a move to expel all Palestinians from Kuwait. Sami and Jihod were both Palestinians and didn't know what to do. They had little money and didn't know how they were going to be able to support themselves.

Although I was aware there was some talk to expel the Palestinians from Kuwait, I personally thought it would be an absolute disaster. The Kuwaitis would have to import a whole new workforce, and the Palestinians would really not have a place to go. It made no sense. I just couldn't imagine the Kuwaitis going through with such a harebrained idea. I tried to calm down Sami and Jihod, but she kept going on about how they didn't have a place to go and that Kuwait was their home.

After about half an hour I told them that if the Kuwaitis were dumb enough to expel all the Palestinians, I would help them come to America. They could both stay at my house for as long as needed to get acclimated, and if necessary, we would hire both of them in our development or construction companies so they would have jobs and thereby be able to get green cards.

Sami reached over, grabbed me around the neck, and kissed me on the cheek. Both Sami and Jihod were overwhelmed by my offer. These were people whom I had met for the first time that day, and they thought my offer was the most generous thing that had ever happened to them. Sami and Jihod now had a contingency plan if things didn't work out in Kuwait. They really were in disbelief.

I didn't know how much money Sami and Jihod made, but I didn't think it was that much. As an afterthought I asked, "Samia, how much do you and Jihod have in the bank?"

They replied, "Almost $650,000."

Now I was the one who was speechless. Sami had

been going on and on all this time about how little they had and how they were going to be poor and destitute for the rest of their lives, and then suddenly I found out they had accumulated more cash than probably 99 percent of Americans would ever accumulate in their lives! We're talking about two working people who were probably not even forty years old yet.

I told Sami, "You and Jihod do not have anything to worry about. Things will work out."

With that, we sat down to eat.

WOMEN IN KUWAIT

In my dealings with the Kuwaitis, I really tried to understand them. One thing I don't think I'll ever understand is why Kuwaiti women who were educated in the US or Europe ever return to the Middle East. Women's rights are nonexistent; there was no women's liberation there.

By most Western standards, the women were verbally and physically abused and were treated as second-class citizens in Kuwait, something I don't understand because of the strong family bonds in Kuwaiti culture. I treat my dog better than I saw some of the Kuwaiti men treating their women. Women do not have the rights that are common in the US and European countries.

The Kuwaiti women I spoke to were generally well educated. Maybe it was a religious thing I didn't understand. The women were absolutely subservient to men. It never made sense to me why virtually all the women went back to Kuwait after schooling outside of the country. Maybe they were afraid of retaliation against themselves or their family members.

GOVERNMENT JOBS

In 1982, standard government working hours in Kuwait were from 7:30 a.m. to 1:30 p.m. Saturday through Wednesday and 7:30 to 11:30 a.m. on Thursdays. A lot of Kuwaitis worked substantially fewer hours. I met many Kuwaiti officials who typically didn't go into the office until 9:30 or 10:00 a.m., left between 11:00 and noon for lunch, and then didn't return for the rest of the day.

But incredibly, a Kuwaiti could retire after five years of working for the government at 75 percent of his highest salary! Retirement payments started immediately and were not impacted by another job or outside source of income.

It became apparent very quickly that most Kuwaitis were not hard workers or driven like a lot of US businessmen. The Kuwaitis liked to do deals but they usually were not involved in a lot of the direct work or details. They were the management or in an ownership position.

The Palestinians, who were typically substantially poorer than the Kuwaitis—even if they did have $650,000 in the bank like my friends Sami and Jihod—performed most of the real work in Kuwait. Many Palestinians were imported to Kuwait as cheap labor.

Palestinians normally lived by their wits, and many had prospered in Kuwait. The ones I met were routinely much less formally educated, but light years ahead of the Kuwaitis in street smarts. Many of the Palestinians I met had excellent minds that assimilated information very quickly in the process of making a decision. Most of them embraced the Kuwaitis' ideals of "Live and let live" and "Don't rock the boat." In comparing the Kuwaitis and Palestinians, I found both groups very approachable, but the Kuwaitis appeared to be more open and forthcoming with information.

PARTING OF THE SEA

On my first trip to Kuwait, Mahmoud recommended that I go over to the gold exchange. I didn't know Kuwait even had a gold exchange! When I went over there, I expected to see a commodities-type exchange, similar to the Chicago Commodities Exchange.

I was absolutely stunned to see one square block filled

with small retailers selling only gold jewelry, coins, and bullion. Think of shops two to six hundred square feet with garage doors that closed to lock the front of the stores. The amount of displayed gold was breathtaking. There were lots of gold necklaces that looked like something Cleopatra might wear. The necklaces were huge, bulky, and probably very heavy. Given the quantity, I had to assume they were selling some of this garish jewelry. I walked around gawking in disbelief that people would buy it.

The gold market was as crowded as a shopping mall at Christmas. The next thing I knew, the sea of people parted. I looked up to see three Bedouin princesses moving through the opening. Sheer black silk completely covered their bodies from head to foot except for diamond cut-outs around their eyes. When I say it was a parting of the sea, that's exactly what it was. Nobody wanted to touch these women because of the consequences, which could be quick and severe. A 280-pound bodyguard trailed them, and he looked like he could play tackle for the Green Bay Packers. As quickly as the princesses arrived, they were gone.

On my many trips to Kuwait, I did not see a lot of really attractive women. This trio of princesses was one of the sexier things I saw in Kuwait.

Of course, being in Kuwait for almost two weeks by that time might have had something to do with it.

THE FOOD MARKET

During my first visit to Kuwait, Mahmoud asked if I wanted to go to the market.

I said, "Sure."

The vendors sold their produce like a large farmers market in the US, but the quality of fresh fruits and vegetables was outstanding. In fact, it was the nicest I have ever seen. It seemed like almost every vendor wanted to give us samples. Based on my one experience in the market, you could probably eat for free just by having daily samples.

Some areas of the market were particularly interesting. In an area where they sold feta, there must have been thirty stalls lined up one after the other, all selling the same type of cheese. Surprisingly, there was a noticeable difference in taste between many of the samples I tried. Some were really outstanding.

We walked past the meat area, where freshly skinned lamb carcasses were hung up on display with no refrigeration. I couldn't believe it. Mahmoud said the meat typically sold so quickly that hanging unrefrigerated meat wasn't a problem. I'm still not sure about that one.

In the seafood area, stalls were filled with piles of different-sized shrimp, although most would be classified as jumbo or colossal. A lot of the shrimp were fifteen-count to maybe even three-count per pound; they really were big. Many varieties of fish could be found, with large Hamour—a type of grouper—being the most prevalent. Hamour was my favorite fish in Kuwait. The seafood was typically caught in the Arabian Gulf nearby, so most of the seafood in restaurants was very fresh.

As previously mentioned, the produce was absolutely first class. Most of it came from Lebanon, although there was a limited amount of locally grown produce from greenhouses which I believe were predominately located in northern Kuwait.

PARKING GARAGE VERSUS MERCEDES

Since it was my first time in Kuwait, I decided to rent a luxury car because of the type of people I thought I would be dealing with. I ended up renting a nice upgraded Mercedes.

The first time I used a parking garage, I was running a little late to a meeting. I parked on what I thought was the fourth or fifth floor of the garage. After my meeting, I realized I hadn't paid enough attention to where I had parked the rental car. No problem. I'm in a Mercedes, so

I'll just look for a dark-colored Mercedes.

I got out on the fourth floor of the parking garage and couldn't believe what I saw. Every car on that floor except one—and there were about eighty cars—was a Mercedes, and most were dark-colored! After checking the whole floor, car by car, I went to the fifth floor.

The fifth floor was almost identical to the fourth floor, although there were probably fifteen fewer cars and four or five of those cars were not Mercedes. After walking the floor twice and not finding my rental, I really started to panic. I had not written down the license plate number of the Mercedes, I couldn't find it on the key chain, nor could I find a telephone number, and I had left my rental car agreement in the glove box.

I went up another level. About halfway through the sixth floor, I found my rental car. In the process, I had wasted about an hour and a half, not counting the anxiety I had put myself through. The good news was I learned a lesson that I've remembered to this day. Whenever I rent a car, I write down the license plate number and put it in my wallet before I leave the rental lot. That tip could save you a lot of future aggravation.

THE PROPHET'S BIRTHDAY

When I visited Kuwait in 1983, Mahmoud wanted me

to attend a celebration for the Prophet's birthday.

I asked, "Will all the businesses be closed?"

Mahmoud replied, "Yes."

"Then I'll be happy to go." Jeez Louise, I couldn't do any business anyway.

I really didn't know what to expect. Maybe there would be a parade downtown and we would wander through a bazaar eating and buying trinkets.

Wrong!

The next morning Mahmoud picked me up at about ten and we drove along the coastal highway for maybe fifteen minutes. We passed large beach houses on pilings that looked like the second-home beach houses you would see along the Texas coast. They were not fancy from the outside. Mahmoud slowed down and turned into one of them. Turned out it was the beach house of one of Mahmoud's wealthy relatives.

Before we got out of the car, Mahmoud said, "Ben, please do not tell my cousin that you are Jewish because I don't know how he would react." In all the time I spent with Mahmoud, this was the only time he ever told me not to say anything about being Jewish. He told me it probably wouldn't be a problem, but if it was, he didn't want to make a scene in front of the large group of people who would be there.

I told him I wouldn't say anything. Then I said, "Mahmoud, tell me about your cousin."

"He is extremely wealthy and very powerful within the Kuwait government," Mahmoud replied. "He is not someone you want pissed off at you."

With that, we got out of the car and walked up the steps to the beach house. The house was probably twenty-five hundred square feet on one level, and most of it was as one large open room. The furnishings were spartan, really basic stuff. There seemed to be thirty men inside already, and another ten to fifteen came later. There were no women or children, and I could hear both English and Arabic being spoken.

Mahmoud introduced me to his cousin and a number of other people, none of whom I specifically remember. As we walked around, I noticed something in Arabic that was framed and hanging on a wall. It was about three feet tall and a foot and a half wide.

I asked Mahmoud, "What is this?"

He said, "It is the family tree going back to the twelfth or thirteenth century."

"That is impressive," I said. "My wife's family can trace their history back to the early 1700s, but I don't know anybody who can trace their family history back to the twelfth or thirteenth centuries."

The people were gathered into small groups, talking mostly about business and current events. I talked for a while with some of the people in two of these informal groups. I didn't know what was cooking in the kitchen, but it sure as hell smelled good.

About that time, several men came out and placed a number of tablecloths on the floor in a long line. And then food came out on large platters. There were a couple of grilled half lambs, a few large Hamour, platters of grilled chicken, vegetables, rice, hummus, pita bread, and buttermilk. There were no eating utensils or plates. The good news was that there were cloth napkins. Everyone then sat down on the floor on each side of the feast. A prayer was said, and everybody started to eat using their hands.

It seemed that every time I was around people from the Middle East, I experienced something new or different, and that was one of those moments. I only remember eating on the floor twice before—once to celebrate Chinese New Year and once at a luau—but I don't remember ever eating everything without utensils. I watched the others for a bit and then dug in. Mahmoud poured me a large glass of buttermilk, which is absolutely not one of my favorites. In fact, I hate buttermilk.

I looked at the buttermilk, knowing that if I didn't

drink it, I would offend Mahmoud. Should I sip it or take my medicine all at one time? So I picked up the glass (which was probably sixteen ounces) and drained the whole damned thing while thinking *yuck, yuck, and yuck,* and then set the glass down.

Mahmoud, apparently thinking I really liked the stuff, poured me another glass before I could say anything. Good grief! This glass remained full throughout the remainder of the meal.

I have to admit that the lamb and Hamour were absolutely outstanding. Of course, I was initially a little uncomfortable reaching my hand into a twenty-five pound fish and tearing off some meat to eat while other people did the same. I might mention this was the only time I was ever at a Kuwaiti's private residence and not offered liquor. No one was drinking. I didn't know if this was specifically because of the Prophet's birthday or if Mahmoud's cousin didn't drink.

After lunch, a couple of groups started playing a card game that I think was called Old Shoe. It was similar to Boo Ray but much simpler. It was played with partners, but it seemed to me that there was virtually no strategy. You just played the cards. Since I grew up playing most card games, I decided to give it a shot. Mahmoud's cousin decided he wanted to be my partner, which I wasn't sure was such a good idea since I had never played the game. But beginners luck prevailed, and we won a few games.

After a couple of hours, I decided I needed to take a walk for some fresh air. I asked Mahmoud to join me. We walked around the property, which was probably an acre in size, and then along the beach.

Mahmoud said, "How much would a place like my cousin's beach house cost in the Houston area?"

I said, "Down on the Bolivar Peninsula it would probably be $125,000, maybe $150,000 on the water."

Mahmoud asked, "Do you have any idea how much my cousin's beach house is worth?"

I replied, "I have no idea."

He said, "Fifteen to twenty times that. Land is extremely expensive in Kuwait."

I could buy a mansion in River Oaks, the nicest residential area of Houston, for that kind of money! I said, "Mahmoud, the land prices are crazy here if that's normal."

He said, "It is normal."

We went back to the house and said our goodbyes at the end of yet another Middle Eastern experience. This time there had been no shopping or parade, but I had had a good time—other than the damned buttermilk. *Yuck! Yuck! Yuck!*

MAHMOUD'S TEA PLANS

Whenever I traveled to Kuwait, Mahmoud Al Adasani would invite me to his house for tea in the morning.

Mahmoud would ask me, "Who do you want to see today?"

I might say, "I'd like to speak to the secretary of the treasury and the president of the one of the large Kuwaiti banks."

I'm telling you, an hour later I would be meeting with the secretary of treasury. This was not "make an appointment for next week," or meeting with some flunky lower down the food chain. There was nobody I asked to see that I didn't get in to see immediately as long as they were in the country.

As an example, on one trip I told Mahmoud I wanted to speak to someone with Funds for Future Generations. The country of Kuwait transferred some money to this fund for every barrel of oil it sold. The growing funds would be used for the Kuwaiti people when the country ran out of oil in the future. And with over $87 billion in the fund already, assuming there were six hundred thousand Kuwaiti citizens and 1.4 million imported workers, I calculated that the fund already had accumulated $145,000 for every Kuwaiti man, woman, and child. Assuming no additional money was ever put into the fund, and the fund could reasonably expect to double the existing money every ten years, I estimated that a hundred years from now there would be over $148 million for every Kuwaiti citizen.

An hour after making my request, we were meeting with Fahad Mohamed Al Rashed, the managing director of the Kuwait Investment Authority which oversaw Funds for Future Generations. After we talked for a half hour, someone came in and whispered in Fahad's ear.

Fahad immediately got up and said, "The emir asked me to meet with three gentlemen from Sudan who are looking for a handout. My apologies. I will be happy to meet with you tomorrow to continue our conversation."

Then he was gone. I thought he had just blown me off and that was the last time I would see him.

Later, about 5:30 p.m., I was watching the news on TV in my hotel room, and there was Fahad and these three gentlemen from Sudan. Fahad was handing them a check for what I thought was $10 million, but it could have been Kuwaiti dinars, and if so, it was $34 million. About that time, I got a call from Fahad apologizing again and asking if I could meet him at nine the next morning at his office.

After thinking about this for a millisecond I said, "I'll be there." After I hung up the phone I started thinking,

Only in Kuwait.

I slept well realizing Fahad hadn't blown me off and that he was not only willing to meet with me tomorrow, but willing to personally call me. In reality, I would have canceled just about any other meeting to meet with Fahad again.

The next morning surpassed my wildest expectations. We met for over three hours. The bottom line: I was going to put an apartment fund together to build apartments in Houston. I would contact one of Fahad's relatives who headed the New York investment office for the Kuwait Investment Authority, because Fahad said they would fund the total $25 million deal.

Now that was an exciting outcome! When I had gone to meet Fahad that morning, I had no idea I might get involved in building apartments.

When I returned to Houston, I spent six weeks putting together the package and lining up people. I had the proposal professionally leather bound with marbleized paper. It was one of the nicest presentations I've ever made. I overnighted the deal to Fahad's relative in New York.

About a week later, a gentleman from New York called to tell me the deal had been approved and they would fund the total $25 million. Then he said he wanted $1 million up front as his fee. I told him I didn't do that. I would be happy to pay him the million out of the $25 million of funding. He said that was unacceptable because he didn't want the Kuwaiti government to know about it.

I said, "Thank you for considering the deal. If you can figure out another way to structure the deal where you are comfortable being paid out of our funding, we would be open. If not, I don't see us doing this deal."

The deal was never funded. Some days it's chicken and some days it's feathers.

TRUTH AND HOSPITALITY

In 1983, during my second trip to Kuwait, I traveled with a Palestinian man whom we will call Fuad Al Said. One day Fuad said that we had been invited to a Kuwaiti's house for dinner the next day. "Do not eat anything before we go tomorrow."

So I fasted all day and drank only water. I was starving by six that evening, but Fuad had told me not to eat. About 8:30 p.m. we finally left to go to the Kuwaiti's house. Unfortunately, I don't remember whose home it was. It could have belonged to one of the Al Bader family members, possibly the Al Bahar family or Al Mustafa family. I just don't remember.

The home was equivalent in size to of one of the largest homes in Houston. A young man who appeared to be in his late teens greeted us at the front door. Fuad and he greeted each other in Arabic, and then the young man said, "Follow me."

He led us into a large diwaniya room—a business reception area. There were probably a hundred people there—men, women, and children—ranging in age from less than a year to probably ninety or older. I could hear Arabic, German, and French, but no English.

The young man motioned for us to sit and asked what I wanted to drink.

I hesitated because I didn't know if he meant water, tea, or hard liquor.

He then asked me in English, "Would you like scotch?"

I said, "That would be fine."

He then asked, "What brand?"

"What do you have?"

"Almost any brand you want."

"Would you please just bring me a single-malt scotch?"

Fuad asked for something in Arabic, and the young man left.

I was really surprised that no one else had come over to greet us or introduce us to the other people. The drinks came and I took a swig. Very nice. I didn't know which single-malt scotch it was, but I was thinking this could become my regular. That is, if I could afford it! It wouldn't have surprised me to learn it was a hundred-year-old scotch. At that point I think my stomach growled, reminding me that I had not eaten all day.

No one tried to engage Faud or me in conversation, and the people there continued their own conversations as if we weren't even in the room. This continued for two hours, with Fuad and me drinking and everybody else speaking Arabic and other foreign languages. I understood absolutely nothing other than when Fuad said something to me in English.

After a couple of hours, an old geezer stood up on the other side of the room. Instantly, everyone else in the place got up. There was immediate silence. The old man crossed the diwaniya room, took me by the arm, and led me into the dining room without saying a word. He sat down and gestured for me to sit on his right. The dining table only seated ten people. Fuad and seven other men filled the other eight seats. There were no women. In fact, it was as though the women and children had vanished off the face of the earth. I didn't see any women or children or hear their voices the rest of the night. I'm also not sure what happened to all the other men who had been in the diwaniya room with us.

Men in their late teens to thirties served the ten people seated at the table. The meal was like a Thanksgiving feast with turkey, lamb, fish, probably ten vegetables, rice, salads, hummus, pita bread, and, later on, a sweet honey-covered pastry like baklava. There was no way I could eat everything, but I tried. The food was really well prepared and tasty.

In Arabic, my host asked me a lot of questions about Houston and the real estate market, which were translated to English by Fuad. He specifically wanted to know what I thought about the economic outlook in Houston for the next five to ten years.

I said, "We have always had a very cyclical real estate market, and the outlook for the next three or four years is excellent. Unfortunately, we have a way of doing everything in excess in Houston, thereby overbuilding the markets from time to time. That usually results in a downward market for probably one to three years before another boom. The booms usually lasted two to three times as long as the total down periods."

My guest was impressed and surprised. Through Faud, he said, "Everyone I previously spoke to about Houston only talked about how great the market is. They didn't mention that it might go down."

That was one of the major lessons I learned about dealing with the Arabs: always tell them the bad with the good because everyone else was blowing smoke up their rears and only telling them the good stuff.

The patriarch suddenly said good night and went to bed. After dinner we adjourned to the library or study with the younger men. It was nice. Fine, dark woodblock paneling that looked like walnut covered the walls. There were bookshelves, a large desk, and two sitting areas that we combined into one by moving some of the furniture around so we could all sit and talk together.

One of my guest's sons asked if I would like some cognac.

I said, "That would be great."

There were now about fifteen men in our group, talking. Most of the men spoke excellent English. One of them suggested we smoke cigars, so cigars were brought out and everyone lit up Cuban cigars. The cognac came and it was superb. I asked the son what type it was, and he said a name I didn't recognize. It didn't matter because I probably couldn't have afforded it anyway.

We sat and talked, drank, and smoked for the next five and a half hours. Among all the people there, we must have solved just about every problem in the world. You know when you hear people talking about a smoke-filled room? Well, this was it. How I made it through without passing out, I'll never know.

At about six in the morning, Fuad and I returned to

our hotel. I'm not sure either of us remembered how we got there in one piece.

LUNCHING IN ARABIAN NIGHTS

Another time, Fuad and I received an invitation to have lunch at a wealthy Kuwaiti's home. We arrived at about twelve thirty with a threatening sandstorm nearby. The man and woman were gracious hosts, and very apologetic, which I did not understand.

Our host told us about a number of planned major real estate projects in Kuwait. Some had been announced and some had not. I was surprised at how open the Kuwaitis appeared to be in telling me things that were not public knowledge. The host and hostess spoke excellent English and were well educated. They also appeared to be quite up to date on world events. In general, most of the Kuwaitis I dealt with were better informed and interested in world affairs compared to the average American businessmen I had met.

After we had a nice lunch, the host said, "I want to show you something."

We followed him out the back door of the home, and there was a huge tent that looked like a circus tent maybe fifteen feet from the house. We went inside, and it looked like it was out of The Arabian Nights. There were silk cushions all around the floor and a low dining table.

The host had set this up for us, but because of the threatening sandstorm, he and his wife thought it would be better to eat inside.

This was all pulled together for the afternoon lunch Fuad and I had with our hosts. There were no other people. They said they would take the tent down the next day after the threat of the sandstorm had passed.

I was overwhelmed—a common occurrence, it seemed, in dealing with the Kuwaitis)

CAMEL BURGER

I have always liked falafel, which is ground chickpeas or fava beans or sometimes a combination. The ground beans are typically rolled into balls, or sometimes small patties, and fried. You then eat them dipped in tahini sauce or in a pita sandwich, which might include lettuce, tomato, mushrooms, onions, fried eggplant, cauliflower, or tahini sauce.

In 1984, on my third trip to Kuwait, I discovered falafel venders with small street stalls sold fresh, excellent falafel sandwiches on the cheap. I could buy a falafel sandwich and cold soft drink for one Kuwaiti dinar—about $3.40 USD at the time. That was only 10 percent or less of what I normally paid for lunch! What a deal. Not only that, in many cases I enjoyed the falafel sandwiches more than the buffets.

But a falafel sandwich just isn't the same as a hamburger.

If you are like me, when you travel overseas for a while you get homesick for an American hamburger, particularly when you've been overseas for three or four weeks. Well, on one of my trips to Kuwait I had reached that critical point after almost three weeks.

I started asking Kuwaitis, "Where are the best burgers?"

Most of the initial answers I received pointed to the US and UK.

So I asked, "Where are the best burger joints in Kuwait City?" The most common response was a blank stare, followed by "None."

Then I started asking people if they knew of any place I could buy a hamburger.

After an hour of asking, I finally got two people to name the same restaurant. I should have known better, but I went to look for this hamburger joint. I was on a burger mission.

From the outside, it looked like a small rundown dump with Arabic on the windows. This could be the Holy Grail of Kuwaiti burger joints. It was definitely dumpy enough. It had all the earmarks of a great burger joint. I went in, sat down, and quickly realized the place was dimly lit. Although I really didn't speak Arabic, I've always been able to order off the menu because I had memorized certain Arabic words on a menu, like *shrimp, lamb,* and *beef.* I might not know how it was prepared, but I got the meat or vegetables I ordered.

It took my eyes a couple of minutes to acclimate to the dim light. I didn't know if some of the lightbulbs had gone out and not been replaced, if it was just poor lighting, or if they planned it that way to cut down on electricity costs. I never considered it was dimly lit for the ambience, which was really lacking. One thing was for sure: I didn't remember ever eating in a good hamburger joint that was dimly lit. The lighting, or lack thereof, was a bad sign.

Finally, my eyes adjusted, and I was barely able to see the menu. I scoured the menu for beef and then hamburger, but I saw neither. I went over the menu again. Nada. As fate would have it, the waiter spoke no English.

I asked, "Do you serve hamburgers?"

Blank stare.

I asked, "Hamburger?" Blank stare again.

I said, "Burger?"

At this, the waiter made a face as if he understood and nodded. I ordered a soft drink, and the waiter vanished into the darkness. I wasn't sure how to read this situation. Maybe they just made it difficult to order a good hamburger.

My soft drink came, and I downed it over a fifteen-minute period and ordered another. After twenty-five minutes I caught the waiter and motioned with my hand toward my lips like I was eating something. He brought me another soda. I shook my head no and pointed to my stomach. He nodded and left.

I was expecting him to be back quickly. So much for expectations in a Kuwaiti hamburger joint. This was not a good sign. He came by my table again fifteen minutes later. I made the same motion, pointing to my stomach and making a chewing motion with my mouth. He nodded and left.

Finally, five minutes later—forty-five minutes after I entered the restaurant—my hamburger arrived, and he placed it on the table in front of me.

I stared at the burger in disbelief. The bun was about ten inches in diameter, and it didn't look like any hamburger bun I had ever seen. It looked like double-thick matzo—unleavened Jewish bread that tastes like cardboard on a good day. It held a small piece of lettuce that was three inches by two inches in size and a slice of tomato that was an inch and a half thick. No mustard or mayo.

The *pièce de résistance* was the meat. If you've ever seen a real Italian meatball, it was like that, but bigger—three and a half inches in diameter. Even in the dim light I could tell this sorry excuse for a burger had been through hell. I've never tried to eat a charcoal briquette before, but if I had, I doubt if there would have been much difference. The briquette would probably have been easier to eat. The first bite was tough and chewy. I tried a second bite and realized it had to be a camel burger. I got up, paid my bill—$26—and left as a very disillusioned hamburger patron.

One good thing did come out of this venture. I swore it was going to be a long time before I ordered another hamburger in Kuwait City. And to this day, I never have.

LAMB'S FEET

Over the years, I have actually come to enjoy good lamb. (Far more than I enjoy camel!) Consistently, the best lamb I've eaten has been prepared in Kuwait and the UK, although I have never been to Australia or New Zealand, so the jury is out on their quality of lamb. I don't know if it is the freshness of the meat or the seasoning, or possibly the way it's grilled or the type of wood they use to cook the lamb. Whatever it is, I highly recommend the lamb in Kuwait. I think that during the 1980s, Kuwait imported most of its lamb live from Australia and New Zealand. Maybe that was why it was so good.

But as much as I enjoy lamb, there was only one time I ever tried lamb's *feet*. I believe it was on my second trip to Kuwait that I met a very personable real estate broker by the name of Abdul Al Jumah. He and I hit it off and started trying to do a couple of real estate deals together. A week later he called my hotel because he wanted me to meet him and some clients for lunch the next day.

We met at a restaurant I was not familiar with. Abdul introduced me to four other gentlemen. These men had purchased some land overlooking the Pacific just south of Los Angeles and were having some zoning issues. Abdul told them I could possibly solve their problem or at least help since I was a knowledgeable real estate developer in the US.

Before I addressed the issue, I told the people a story. When I started subdivision development in the Houston area, it was fun. There was limited governmental interference, and basically, I acted as a problem solver on the front end. It was not much different from putting a puzzle together or working a crossword puzzle. Mentally it was challenging to make something work that others couldn't, and it also was ego satisfying. But after a while, I questioned whether Houston was the best place to develop because there were a lot of other large markets in the US with better climates.

After some serious research I narrowed the possibilities to Florida and California. I went to Florida, where I spent the better part of a month researching land development and talking to builders, developers, engineers, and government employees in different agencies. I then went to southern California for about three weeks doing the same thing. When I got back to Houston and analyzed my findings, I determined the following:

In Florida, to do a Development of Regional Impact (DRI) and get the necessary governmental approvals to develop would, on average, take a year and a half, not counting my time and the cost. That would be the average time before you could turn the first spade of dirt for the development.

In California, there were even more rules and regulations than in Florida. The red tape was mind-boggling. The same type of development that would take a year and a half in Florida would take approximately five years in California.

In Houston, the same type of land development, including getting all governmental approvals might take thirty days, so you can understand why I develop in Houston.

Now, to address their issue. They were having problems rezoning land they wanted to develop into nineteen single-family residential lots. It was currently zoned for five. I told them, based upon my previous experience in dealing in California, that they had major problems unless they planned to be in the deal for two to five additional years and were prepared to go to court and pay the resulting legal fees.

I said I thought they were in a Coastal Conservation District that was staffed by former Environmental Protection Agency (EPA) personnel who wanted to save the world and would fight them tooth and nail. It was immaterial that they legally had the right to rezone the property into nineteen lots. The EPA people would throw up every roadblock and delaying action in the book.

The bureaucrats figured time was on their side. The average developer did not have the money or fortitude to sue them because it was costly, time consuming, and could take two to five years or possibly longer. I suggested they approach a local developer with a good reputation to see if they would get the same recommendation.

They were absolutely stunned. There was silence at the table.

Finally, one of the men table said, "Our real estate broker told us we could do this easily."

I said, "Your real estate broker was pulling the wool over your eyes to make the sale."

Again, there was silence at the table.

I then suggested they sell the property if they could and reinvest their money in another deal. If it was to be in California, I suggested they buy a property that had absolutely all approvals in writing from all the appropriate governmental agencies ahead of time.

After some talk in Arabic among the partners, the lead person said, "What you just told us is not what we wanted to hear, but it sounds like you are knowledgeable and telling us the truth, since you have no interest in this deal. We will take your recommendation under advisement."

At that point they decided to celebrate because they had finally agreed upon a course of action. One of the men ordered in Arabic. He told me he had ordered something special for me. I thanked him, but my curiosity got the better of me. I asked, "What did you order?"

He replied, "Lamb's feet."

Well, I'd eaten lamb before, but never had lamb's feet. I had tried pickled pig's feet, which were all right. I have a cast-iron stomach and was adventuresome in my eating habits. I would try just about anything once, and I liked most of the food I had had in Kuwait. They had exceptionally good grilled meats and fish.

What could be so bad about lamb's feet? Little did I know . . .

Because of nasal allergies and other problems, I did not, and currently do not, have a good sense of smell. Despite that, about ten minutes later, I started to smell this really foul odor coming from the direction of the kitchen. If I could smell it, normal people should be gagging and passing out but nobody said anything.

Finally I asked, "Do you smell a strong odor?"

One of the guys said, "Don't worry. It's normal."

I was starting to feel uncomfortable when suddenly two waiters appeared, one of them carrying a huge platter of lamb's feet that he placed in the middle of our table. The odor was absolutely obnoxious. Without saying anything, everyone else at the table grabbed a lamb's foot and dug in. I don't know if you've ever looked at a lamb's foot before, but there is no meat.

No meat.

These guys went through lamb's feet like chicken wings. The only difference was they were eating the gelatinous mass and cartilage, leaving a few small bones.

One of the guys said, "The lamb's feet are really good. You ought to try one. You don't know what you are missing."

What the heck. When in Rome do as the Romans do.

So I took a bite.

Big mistake.

It wasn't just bad; it was the worst thing I have ever put in my mouth by far, although I eat almost anything and, yes, I'd had a lamb's eyeball before. To this day I will not eat lamb's feet. In fact, I don't even want it on a table where I'm sitting.

And, no, I never did any business with these guys.

THE GIFT OF DALGEE

Even back home in Houston, I kept getting new introductions to Kuwaiti traditions—some of them shocking. This is another one of those totally astonishing stories that I wouldn't believe if it hadn't happened to Bill and me.

Ahmed had a limo driver by the name of Dalgee who also was a bodyguard, did odd jobs for him, and ran errands. My partner and I liked Dalgee. One afternoon Ahmed came to our offices to speak to us. I was tied up in a meeting, so Ahmed met with Bill.

Ahmed told Bill that he was going back to Kuwait and he was giving Dalgee to us.

My partner asked, "What do you mean, you're giving us Dalgee?"

Ahmed said, "I bought Dalgee when he was two and have owned him ever since. You and Ben are good people, and I am sure you will treat Dalgee well. I hereby give you Dalgee."

With that, Ahmed left.

Bill was flabbergasted. He didn't know how to respond. As soon as my meeting was over, he rushed into my office.

"You better be sitting down because we have a problem."

I asked, "What's up?"

"Ahmed just gave us Dalgee."

I said, "Great, I was thinking that he could drive the limo and run errands because he is completely reliable and trustworthy."

Bill said, "No, you don't understand. Ahmed just *gave* us Dalgee."

I said, "Okay. What's the big deal?"

Bill said, "We now *own* him."

I said, "Like we're going to put him on the payroll?"

Bill said, "We fricking *own* him! Ahmed bought Dalgee when he was very young, and he just gave Dalgee to us."

I just stared at him in utter disbelief. The computer in my mind was saying, *Does not compute, does not compute.* I was speechless. Stuff like this didn't happen in the US. Maybe my partner was pulling a fast one on me. I said, "Good one."

"I ain't fricking joking. Ahmed just gave us Dalgee. What do we do?"

I didn't have a clue. "Can we undo it and not take Dalgee?"

"Are you fricking crazy?"

No wonder my partner was so agitated. This couldn't be real. We really owned Dalgee!

After a few minutes of utter shock, we decided that we needed to go meet with Michael O'Brien, our former attorney who was now a Texas state judge.

I don't think we even made an appointment; we just went to his office. We explained the situation and he quieted us down. He said the answer was to contact an immigration attorney and get Dalgee a green card, allowing him to legally work in the US, and then citizenship.

We met with Dalgee and explained to him that he was free. We did not own him, and we would do everything we could to make him legal so he could stay in the US.

As I remember, we spent ten grand trying to get Dalgee legal over many months. We had major problems trying to establish a birth certificate. In the end, one of our secretaries married Dalgee and solved our problem.

We really had great secretaries!

TWO BOTTLES OF LAFITE ROTHSCHILD

About those secretaries. We had a number of very young, attractive ladies working for us. They were regularly approached by our Arab clients about going out with them. Some said *yes* and some said *no*.

Ann Powel, an attractive blonde, headed our title company. She met one of our Arab clients at a real estate closing she handled. The Saudi prince was interested in Ann, but Ann had no interest in him. One afternoon, shortly after the closing, a limo driver came to Ann's office and asked her to go downstairs with him. She followed him to find a stretch limo waiting with the Saudi prince. The prince handed her two bottles of vintage Lafite Rothschild wine and asked her to call him.

For those of you not familiar with Lafite Rothschild wine, it is arguably one of the best known and most expensive red wines in the world. When France rated its best wines in 1855, Lafite Rothschild was rated a first-growth—the best, of which there were only four. The wine probably cost the equivalent of half a month's salary for Ann.

Ann never called the prince. One evening she made meatloaf for herself and drank some of the Lafite Rothschild. She said it went down really well with her meal!

DISHDASHA DILEMMA

When Mahmoud Al Adasani stayed with us in Houston, he typically wore the traditional *dishdasha* around the house—traditional Arab garb that looks like pajamas—and he wore Western clothes when he went out. I once asked why.

Mahmoud said he found the dishdasha more comfortable and less restrictive than Western clothes. After wearing a dishdasha a few times, I couldn't disagree.

There was a problem with Mahmoud's wearing a dishdasha around the house, though. We had a dog named Motley that was half Labrador retriever and half basset hound. She had short legs like a basset hound and bayed like a hound, but acted like a big lap dog. In fact, Motley was an indoor lap dog that weighed about ninety pounds. Any time a dog came in contact with Mahmoud's dishdasha it was supposed to be washed—nine times, I think—if you followed the faith, and Mahmoud did. Since Motley was a people-loving indoor dog, this presented problems. Mahmoud washed lots of dishdashas and Motley spent a lot of time outside during the day.

Eventually, they reached an uneasy truce with only occasional lapses by Motley when she got excited.

BUYING THE EMIR A GIFT

One fine day in the mid-eighties, Mahmoud Al Adasani called me from New York. He said he was on his way to Las Vegas, but he was stopping in Houston because he needed some help buying the emir of Kuwait a gift.

I said to Mahmoud, "Are you kidding me?"

"No. I'm absolutely serious."

"Sure, I'd be glad to help," I said. At the same time, I was thinking, *What do you buy a fricking king that he can't buy a hundred of?* I didn't see any sections in my resume saying, *Personal shopper for kings!*

I asked Mahmoud when he would arrive, thinking I'd have at least a couple of days.

He asked, "Could you pick me up at Intercontinental Airport in four hours?"

I said, "Sure." But inside, I was slightly panicked.

Mahmoud gave me his flight information and hung up. I immediately called my partner to see if he had any ideas. He suggested something Texan, but he didn't offer any further inspiration. I called a couple of my friends, with even worse results.

The first one said, "I have no idea, but if I think of something, I'll get back to you in a month or two."

That was lots of help since I needed the gift the next day.

I then called a second friend, who responded, "Ben, you're living in fairyland. It took you three months to think of a birthday gift last year for your wife, and now you need to come up with an idea for a neat gift for a king in one day. Is this a joke? Are you pulling my leg?"

I assured him it wasn't a joke.

He was laughing as he hung up the phone and said, "You're screwed."

I already knew that.

I sat there in my office in shock, just staring at the receiver. It wasn't like I knew any kings and could call them for suggestions. Obviously, none of my friends had bought a gift for a king. Whom could I call for ideas? I had no clue and had to pick up Mahmoud in a little over three hours. I poured myself a double Wild Turkey on the rocks. I needed all the help I could get.

I called my Sheri to tell her Mahmoud would be staying with us that night and maybe the next day.

She said, "Terrific!" There was sarcasm in her voice. It wasn't that she minded Mahmoud staying with us; it was the short notice. Unfortunately, there was nothing I could do about that.

I told her I'd stop and get something for supper on our way home. We'd probably be home in about four hours. "Oh, by the way, do you have any ideas for a gift for the emir of Kuwait?"

There was lots of laughter as she hung up.

I really was screwed.

On my drive to the airport, I tried to approach the problem logically. *All right, the emir can buy anything he wants. That's a given. The emir is accustomed to having the best of everything. That is a given. Many of the gifts in the Middle East are garish compared to Western tastes. That is a given. They like gold in the Middle East. That is a given.*

I wasn't sure how much the emir would know about Texas other than oil and cowboys. How about a cowboy hat, cowboy boots, and a leather cowboy belt? Ahmed had sure liked the cowboy attire we gave him. But no, that wouldn't work; I didn't know the emir's sizes.

How about a gun? No, the emir didn't hunt.

I had seen very little art on the walls in Kuwaiti homes, so an oil painting would be a long shot. Food and wine were out. The emir might or might not be interested and knowledgeable about new electronic inventions or gizmos. So they were probably out.

What did that leave?

After thinking about this for ten or fifteen minutes, I decided the gift probably needed to be handmade and unique. How about a pen to sign royal decrees?

No, too common.

How about an intricate, wooden, handmade box?

Maybe . . .

How about a sculpture?

Ah! That might be the answer. Now the question became: if a sculpture, what should it be? Should it be contemporary or traditional? Should it be new or antique? So by the time I picked up Mahmoud, I had a suggestion for a gift. Mahmoud liked the idea of a sculpture.

All right! At least we had an idea for shopping the next day. I felt some relief, but since the gift hadn't been purchased yet, there was still major anxiety.

We stopped at Abdallah's Bakery on Hilcroft near Westpark to pick up Middle Eastern food to go. The bakery had become one of the Arabs' favorite places to eat in Houston, along with Sammy's, a Lebanese restaurant located about half a mile away on Richmond Avenue. We ordered a beef shawarma—sliced rotisserie beef with pickles, onions, and sauce wrapped in pita bread; grilled chicken; a lamb shank with lentils; beef shish kabob; eggplant; labneh—yogurt and sliced dill pickles; Greek salad; cauliflower; tabbouleh—a Middle Eastern salad; hummus—mashed chickpeas and olive oil used as a dip; pita bread; and dates. When we got home, we had a feast.

The next day, I took Mahmoud over to the Galleria, a shopping center in Uptown Houston, to buy a sculpture for the emir. As we walked into the first art store, the first thing I spied was a smaller bronze sculpture of a bald eagle. It was about eighteen inches high and a little over a foot wide. I asked the manager of the art gallery who had made the piece and how many copies had been made.

He told me the name of the sculptor, whom I did not recognize—realistically, he could have told me Yogi Bear; because I didn't know any sculptors anyway—said that it was a new piece, and that it was one of a kind.

I thought it was perfect. Mahmoud agreed. That was it, other than having it gift wrapped and paying $4,000!

You can imagine the great sense of relief that I felt as we left. Another crisis averted.

I assume that sculpture is now in some warehouse in Kuwait gathering dust.

7

POWER

ALL THOSE BUSINESS dealings with Arabs introduced me to men of incredible power. On one of my trips to Kuwait, a real estate broker I had previously met said he had someone he wanted to introduce me to.

I said, "Sure, I'll be happy to meet him." I assumed the man would meet us at the broker's office.

Yeah, right.

We were to meet at the broker's office at two in the afternoon the next day.

I showed up, and the first thing the broker said was, "Are you ready?"

I said I was, not knowing what to expect.

The next thing I knew, we were getting into the broker's Rolls Royce. I assumed we were going to the office of the person this broker wanted me to meet. We rode for about twenty-five minutes with nothing but desert on both sides of the road. He slowed down, turned into the desert, and then started accelerating again. So there we were, in a Rolls Royce going forty-five to fifty miles an hour through the desert, which, by the way, meant there was no fricking road!

I asked the broker, "What the hell are we doing?"

He said, "We're going to meet someone special."

"In the middle of the desert?"

"We are going to meet a mullah."

My heart stopped. "A real mullah?"

"Yes, a mullah."

Mullahs were chieftains who had led their nomadic people through the Arabian Peninsula trading for thousands of years. They did not accept any country's boundaries or law. The local law enforcement and governments didn't bother with them. Period. The mullahs' word was law.

If a mullah decided he wanted you dead, they probably wouldn't find your scorched bones for a hundred years. This is a guy that, if he got pissed off, could blow his ram's horn—or whatever he used—and the next morning, ten thousand men would show up with guns, knives, pitchforks, or whatever weapons they had, prepared to give up their lives for the mullah. You didn't want to say the wrong thing to a mullah—ever!

And I was in the middle of nowhere, in the desert, on my way to meet one.

My hindquarters suddenly closed like a bear trap. What was I doing there? I asked, "Are you sure this is a good idea?"

I'm sure the broker was holding in a laugh as he said, "Sure, there's nothing to worry about. This mullah has some money he wants to invest."

I was thinking, *Does not compute, does not compute!*

Suddenly, in the distance, I see four or five tents.

The broker said, "That's where we are going."

I gulped and immediately started to envision all the bad things that could happen, starting with my being killed. If that didn't happen, I could be sexually assaulted, sold into slavery, or held for ransom. My mind ran wild.

The broker pulled up and said, "We're here."

He got out, but I didn't move. He walked around the front of the car to my side and opened the door. I really didn't want to get out.

He said, "There is nothing to worry about."

I said, "I can wait here."

By the time he finally coaxed me out of the Rolls Royce, a man had come out from one of the tents and was headed our way.

The broker and the man both spoke to each other in

Arabic, and after a greeting, the broker motioned for me to follow them into another tent. One minute I was looking at the exterior of some old, grubby-looking tents, and the next minute I was blinking inside a beautiful hideaway that looked like a canvas palace. People sitting on cushions formed a thirty-foot wide, U-shaped area in the middle of the tent.

We were greeted by two men who escorted us to the mullah, who was seated in the middle. Although he was probably in his mid-seventies, he was not at all what I expected. He looked to be in good shape physically and was bigger than I would have thought. I was expecting someone in his nineties, or older, a frail old man on his last leg.

In Arabic, one of the men asked the broker if we wanted tea. He responded *yes* and asked for no sugar in mine because I was prediabetic. About five minutes later, a tray arrived, with the tea carried by a younger man. Typically, the tea in the Middle East was very strong with a heavy dose of sugar and served in very small glasses. Mine was strong and sugary too. So much for no sugar.

There was a lot of talking in Arabic with no English translations. After twenty minutes or so, the mullah got around to me. He spoke no English, so everything was interpreted. He asked where I was from, and when I told him I was from Houston, Texas, he immediately asked if I was a cowboy and rode a horse. I told him I wasn't a cowboy but I did know how to ride a horse, and that I owned cowboy boots and a cowboy hat.

He found this amusing.

The mullah asked if I found the land there to be too hot. I explained that the temperatures in Houston typically got up to a hundred degrees in the summer and we had high humidity. I said it was a little hotter here, but not bad. He asked if I was married and had children. I told him I was married and had one young daughter and a son on the way.

I asked if the mullah had many children. He smiled and said, "Yes, many."

You know, other than being in the desert, in the middle of nowhere, in a tent speaking to a guy who could have had me killed in a heartbeat and nobody would have done anything about it, the conversation seemed normal. Then he asked why I was there. I told him I was a real estate developer who was doing business with the Al Babtain family and Mahmoud Al Adasani.

He nodded.

At this point, the broker started speaking to the mullah in Arabic. This continued back and forth for around ten minutes. I had absolutely no idea what they were talking about. It could have been business, women, the weather, or slitting my throat. I was clueless.

Suddenly the broker said, "The mullah will think it over and get back to us."

I said, "Huh?"

"It's time to go."

So I said my goodbyes and we left.

As we're riding through the desert in the Rolls Royce I said, "Criminy, what just happened?"

The broker said he had asked the mullah for five million Kuwaiti dinars—about $17 million—on my behalf!

Stunned, I asked, "Why did you do that?"

"To arranged the deal. I will charge you 15 percent for arranging it."

I asked, "Deal? What deal?"

"Raising the money."

"To do what?"

"To invest for him."

"In what?"

"Whatever you want."

"What type of return did you tell him he would get?"

"I didn't tell him any return."

"You mean you just asked someone for $17 million to invest in anything I want without talking about a return and the guy said he would think about it?"

"Yes."

"What happens if he is not happy with his returns?"

And this is a classic response: "There could be consequences."

"Holy moly." I told the broker I appreciated the effort he had just made on my behalf—of course, he would have earned $2.55 million for his own account—but that I thought it would be too risky.

As he turned out of the dessert onto the paved highway heading toward Kuwait City, he asked, "What risk?"

I had to hold in a laugh myself when I said, "You are dealing with a fricking mullah. You don't think there would be an impediment to my doing future business if the mullah was pissed at me?"

"It might lead to a tricky situation."

"A tricky situation, my ass!"

"Well, there might be some consequences."

"Incredible!"

"You're smart," the broker said. "You're not going to lose his money. You've probably been in thornier situations before that you've gotten out of. You'll be able to do it."

"The thorny situations I've been in didn't involve someone trying to slice off my yang or my head."

As we rode the rest of the way mostly in silence, I really wondered, Is this the real world, or have I fallen into some wormhole in space where everything is fairyland?

We ultimately decided to pass on this deal. I can't imagine why.

WARM, WORLDLY, AND KNOWLEDGEABLE

Surreal situations popped up repeatedly during my dealings with Arabs. On my first two-week trip to Kuwait in 1982, I was invited to dinner at a wealthy local architect's home. The home was more modernly designed than most homes I had seen in Kuwait, and among other things, there was a huge indoor swimming pool. There were probably a dozen male guests, including Mahmoud and me. I found the guests most intriguing.

These were not the exact positions or titles of the guests, but this will give you an idea of the type of people attending. There was the head of Public Works for Kuwait City, the president of a large bank, the head of the Air Force, someone in the Secret Service, someone from the royal family, an industrialist involved in manufacturing in over ten countries, two extremely wealthy people who owned a number of multinational companies, the soccer coach of the national soccer team, and a major owner of a very large shipping company that owned freighters and tankers. The host was the head of a major architectural firm building mega projects throughout the whole Gulf region.

The people involved probably represented 15 percent of the major Kuwaiti families who ran the country on a day-to-day basis. Most of the people there spoke better English than I did and had been educated at the best universities in the US and Europe, and many had advanced degrees. Some of the colleges and universities they had attended were Cambridge, the London School of Economics, Harvard, Rice, and MIT.

The host will remain nameless because he was having some slight problems with the government. He had been caught smuggling a whole planeload of liquor into Kuwait! (On a Boeing 707.)

The host and hostess were warm and outgoing people and they were very comfortable to be around. I probably learned more about how things got done in Kuwait at that dinner than at any other meeting on that trip, and I was surprised by how open the people were. They answered my questions without dancing around the issues. The attitude of virtually all the people there was live and let live. They were happy with their lifestyles and didn't want anyone rocking the boat.

I was shocked to learn that virtually everyone there financially supported both the Palestine Liberation Organization (PLO) *and* Israeli causes. They explained to me that when the dust settled, they wanted a winner. Based upon my previous US media exposure, this was completely shocking to my preconceived ideas about the Arabs.

These people were worldly and knowledgeable about a great many things other than business. Items discussed included art, history, gardening, women, woodworking, traveling in Eastern Europe, fishing, working out, immigration, problems with the Palestinians in Kuwait—at that time, I wasn't even aware there was a problem—and many other subjects. I was pleasantly surprised because I was not expecting to meet people who appeared to be so knowledgeable in so many vastly different areas other than business. These people were interesting, willing to think outside the box, and fun to be around.

Many of the people there asked me to stop by their offices later in the week if I had the time.

Are you kidding me? I'll be there!

DIPLOMATIC IMMUNITY—NOT FOR ME

Kuwait has an interesting dichotomy in their society. Many of the Kuwaitis we dealt with drank, smoked, gambled, and chased women, but were also religious, saying their prayers daily. Publicly, they all supported whatever official line the government espoused. Privately, behind closed doors, many of them were diametrically opposed to the public stance of the government. We were in many Kuwaiti homes that were better stocked than your local liquor store.

One of my major concerns in Kuwait was the fact that I was dealing with people who all had diplomatic passports. I was obviously not traveling on a diplomatic passport, and I was constantly concerned that one of our clients might send a woman over to my hotel room. If I was caught with a woman, the best-case scenario would see me immediately deported back to the US. The worst-case scenario could have been major jail time. Like *years*.

The same thing was true about liquor. If I were caught drinking alcohol in the hotel, I would have almost surely been asked to leave the country immediately and not invited back ever again.

MEETING WITH CORPORATE GIANTS

In 1982, on my second trip to Kuwait, I decided I wanted to go by BoodaiCorp. This company had an excellent reputation within the Kuwaiti community. In Kuwait, Boodai exclusively represented Renault, two exotic car companies, Mitsubishi AC units, Nissan and Doltz diesels, Fram filters, and Black & Decker, and they were heavily involved with heavy oilfield equipment, cranes, hand tools, generators, compressors, batteries, and welding supplies, among many other items.

I had gone by to see Marwan Boodai, who turned out to be in London, so, instead, I met with Tarek Abdul Karim, the corporate manager. Although the meeting went well, I got the feeling that Marwan was the real decision maker. We talked about the possibilities of joint venturing subdivision development in the Houston area and about buying distressed properties from lenders. Tarek said that Boodai would be interested in exploring future possibilities with us, but we were never able to get a deal done.

In the last thirty years, BoodaiCorp has grown dramatically in additional areas, including telecommunications, TV, print media, cement, public transportation, commercial aviation, aviation leasing, an airline, logistics, commodities, and engineering services.

On another one of my trips, I met with Al Khonaini Al Katami, who was involved with construction machinery, office furniture, household furnishings, firefighting equipment, waterproofing, building materials, electrical, chemicals, pigments, tires, rubber products, cables, steel pipe, and decorating items. In 2002, the Al Khonaini family bought out the Al Katami family.

During my 1983 visit, I met with Ahmed Abdul Aziz

Al Katami, chairman; James Adas, general manager; and Mona Mohd A Al Khonaini; a member of the board of directors. It was very unusual to find a female in a position of authority in the major Kuwaiti family businesses. I found Mona to be cold, closed in, and very difficult to engage in conversation. On the other hand, the men were much more approachable, including Saif Daher, an engineer I met later who managed their Sino-Kuwait projects. The bottom line was that privately, off the record, Saif said that the only way I was going to be able to do business with Al Khonaini Al Katami was through Mona to Ahmed.

I told him I thought Mona was a cold fish and I didn't think I could successfully deal with her. He understood and wished me luck. He promised to call me if the situation changed.

MEETING THE PLO WITH FAUD

Fuad, my Palestinian friend, told me someone who was equivalent to the treasurer of the Palestine Liberation Organization (PLO) had invited us to lunch. This was in 1983. We met at his home about noon, and the first thing I noticed was the house interior had more of a Western or European feel than most Kuwaiti homes I had seen.

Our host and his wife were among the most gracious people I have ever met. After spending some time with them, I felt that they could have just as easily fit into New York or Houston as they did in the Middle East. The man was well educated, fit, well dressed, up to date on foreign affairs, and spoke multiple languages, including excellent English. He was well spoken, sharp as a tack, and had a good sense of humor.

While we were eating, their son came in wearing his polo outfit. He told us he had just competed in a polo tournament in which his team had done very well. Their son was excitedly talking about a hundred miles per hour. Our host appeared to be extremely proud of his son. I think this family would have been equally comfortable in formal wear or jeans. They really appeared to be a loving, caring family unit.

We had a very nice lunch and talked for hours. What impressed me the most was when I asked our host, "What is it going to take to have peace in the Middle East with Israel?"

His reply showed incredible insight into the problem. He answered that there was a major problem on both sides. "Let's say I was an Arab and went over to Israel and killed an Israeli. Then the Israeli father or brother retaliated and killed two Arabs. Let's say that the father and brother of the slain Arabs then retaliated by killing more Israelis. Unfortunately, this has happened over and over, and the leadership of both Israel and the PLO is predominately composed of hard-liners who have lost friends and relatives. The people most committed to their cause have risen to the top on both sides. The problem is that most of the people on both sides are moderates. If there were some way to strip out the leadership on both sides, there could be a lasting peace."

I thought this was an excellent summation of reality.

The host continued to say that, short of the leadership on both sides being removed, which wasn't going to happen, the solution would have to come through the slow process of education. The only lasting peace would come by dispelling a lot of misinformation on both sides.

He said, "We have to learn together, work together, and prosper together." Without pointing a finger, he said he thought there had been abuses on both sides, and he didn't know how to resolve the issues in the short run. But if a peace agreement were signed, both parties needed to be prepared for short-term breaches in the agreement as radical groups on both sides would try to provoke the other side.

What this man said was absolutely profound and true. The meeting was a real eye-opener for me. All the US media depictions I had seen portrayed the PLO as terror-istic, unreasonable, and poorly educated rabble-rousers. And what I was listening to could just as easily have come from an Israeli scholar or an American. I was shocked to hear these things, but at the same time very pleased. You know, with people like this in the world, there really might be the possibility of a lasting peace in the Middle East for our children and grandchildren.

OFFER TO MEET ARAFAT

As it turned out, Fuad had grown up with Yasser Ara-fat, chairman of the Palestine Liberation Organization, which I did not know when we went to Kuwait together. While we were in Kuwait one day Fuad asked me, "Would you like to go meet Arafat?"

I was stunned.

I asked, "Do you know him?"

Fuad said, "I grew up with him and have known him forever."

I didn't know what to say.

Faud continued with some stories about things they had done together while growing up.

I asked Fuad, "Is Arafat here in Kuwait?"

Faud said, "No, we would have to go meet him some-where, depending on his travel schedule."

After thinking about it, I replied, "Thanks for the offer, but I don't think so now. I'm involved here in Kuwait, and I don't think I would have the time on this trip to take off to meet him, although it sounds interesting."

This was another of those missed opportunities where I should have taken Fuad up on his offer.

MEETING MY LAST MULLAH

After my first meeting with a mullah in the desert, I thought I would never, ever meet another mullah.

Wrong.

As luck would have it, it happened again by total chance. I was waiting for a table at a nice restaurant when a gentleman accidently backed into me, causing me to spill my drink down the front of my shirt.

He apologized profusely and said he wanted to pay for the cleaning and a new drink.

I laughed and declined his nice offer, but said, "Thank you for offering." He didn't do it on purpose, so there was no harm.

He asked me for a business card and gave me one of his.

His card said he worked for the Kuwait government in what sounded like some small, obscure governmental agency. I didn't give it any further thought.

The next afternoon I was in my room at the Sheraton Hotel when there was a knock at my door. I answered the door to see somebody I didn't know.

In perfect English the man said, "The gentleman who bumped into you last night wants to speak to you."

I said, "It isn't necessary. There is no problem from last night, but thank him again for his concern."

He said, "No, you don't understand. He really wants to speak to you."

I didn't understand what all the fuss was about; that was until he flashed his official-looking law enforcement badge and gun and said, "I insist."

I said, "Okay," and my butt cheeks clenched. What could I have done to offend this man? Why was he making such a big deal out of nothing? Did I need to call Mahmoud to get me out of trouble?

And then it hit me: How did he know where I was staying in Kuwait? I hadn't mentioned that I was staying at a hotel or where it was. This could not have been just some minor government official.

We rode in an unmarked Mercedes, and instead of driving downtown, we drove out to a nicer upper-middle-class neighborhood where the houses were probably four to six thousand square feet. He pulled into the driveway of one of the nicer houses and parked.

He said, "Go knock on the door, and I will wait in the car for you."

At least that sounded promising. He planned to take me somewhere after I met this guy for who knows what reason. I got out, went to the front door, and rang the bell.

A gentleman I didn't recognize answered the door and said, "Follow me," in perfect English with a British accent. I then remembered the British had previously had a big presence in this area of the Middle East. I was escorted into a very nice room that looked like an office or study, and asked to sit. There was nobody else in the room. The man closed the door and left.

I waited for about five minutes before the gentleman who had backed into me at the restaurant came in and greeted me.

The first thing he said was, "You have nothing to worry about. You are not in danger."

The old butt cheeks unclenched a little, but not all the way. "Why am I here? This isn't about a spilled drink."

"No," he said. "I work for the government in a small agency that solves problems."

My butt cheeks clenched up again. "What does this have to do with me?"

"Well, we might be able to help each other."

My butt cheeks double clutched as they tightened

some more. "What do you want?"

He said, "We have a situation where we need your help."

I was now feeling very uncomfortable.

The gentleman said, "We have been following a man for a year, and we need entrance to his compound."

"What does that have to do with me?"

"Well, we know you are looking for investors for some of your real estate deals in Houston. We may be able to help. This person has a lot of cash he wants to invest out of the country."

I said, "We're not interested in investing with drug money or people involved in other criminal activities."

The gentleman said, "This person has never been convicted of anything."

I said, "We do not deal in cash. We have turned down a number of investors who have come to our offices with suitcases or briefcases full of cash. If there is not a paper trail through a legitimate bank, lending source, or brokerage account, we are not interested in dealing with them." I continued, "We are absolutely not interested in procuring armament, drugs, laundering money, or doing anything that would possibly be perceived as illegal or immoral, period."

There was silence as the gentleman took all this in.

He then said, "It is refreshing to find a person who says they only take the high road when being offered tens of millions of dollars."

I said, "Find another patsy. We are not interested in doing business with this unnamed person."

The gentleman frowned and said, "If you won't do it for money, would you do it for the government of Kuwait?"

No response from me.

The gentleman said, "Mahmoud was correct when he said you wouldn't do it for money."

"I want to call Mahmoud."

He motioned for me to use the phone.

I called Mahmoud and said, "Mahmoud, are you involved in this deal the government is supposedly trying to get me involved in?"

There was silence for a moment. Finally Mahmoud said, "Our government has a problem that you could possibly help solve for us. I was approached by the gentleman you met last night and asked if I thought you would be willing to help the government of Kuwait. I told him that you probably would, but I didn't think you would do it for money. I assume they offered you lots of money and you turned them down."

I chuckled. Mahmoud knew me better than I thought.

Mahmoud said, "Ben, would you please help us?"

I asked, "Is this something that is going to be dangerous?"

Mahmoud said he didn't think so but he wasn't sure. Although I was still nervous, I said I would try to help. Mahmoud thanked me and asked to speak to the gentleman. I handed the phone back to him. They spoke in Arabic for a few minutes, and then the fellow hung up.

The gentleman said to me, "I am sorry if I offended you, but most businessmen would have gone instantly for the cash."

I nodded.

He continued, "Some of the major Kuwaiti families have said some very nice things about you. I've heard the Texas term 'straight shooter' more than once."

I smiled but didn't say anything.

The gentleman said, "We want to set up a meeting with this person, who is a mullah."

I blanched when he said *mullah*.

He asked, "Are you okay?"

I said, "I'd like some water."

He buzzed someone on the phone and said something in Arabic. Almost instantaneously someone came in with bottled water. I took a long swig.

I then said, "Mahmoud said he didn't think this was dangerous, and I said I'd help. That was before I was told

I would be dealing with a fricking mullah."

The gentleman motioned for me to calm down, as I was getting very agitated. I took a deep breath and tried to relax my butt cheeks, but they wouldn't unclench.

He said, "We want to set up a meeting for you and your entourage with this person to discuss investments. You'll then agree to let one of your entourage travel on with this person's party."

I said, "What entourage?"

He told me they would handle it, but I expressed my discomfort. He understood and said he wouldn't be asking if it weren't necessary.

I asked him to tell me the truth: "Did you accidentally bump into me, or was that on purpose?"

He took a deep breath and said, "It was planned."

Holy crap! My mind was racing a million miles an hour. Was there some graceful way I could get out of this? I sure didn't think of any answers in a timely manner.

The gentleman said, "We'll set up a meeting for tomorrow night. Two of my best men will be going with you, and they will be armed."

I told him, "That really will be reassuring because the mullah will probably only have fifty to a hundred armed men."

He said, "You are right, but you really shouldn't be in

danger."

That was really reassuring!

I said, "I'm tired and want to go back to my hotel." I was absolutely drained. I kept asking myself, *How does this stuff happen to me?*

The next day the gentleman called to say he wanted me to meet his two men and go over the real estate deal to present to the mullah they were concerned about.

That afternoon we met, and I was pleasantly surprised by how sharp his guys were. They already had a good basic understanding of real estate deals, they spoke excellent English, and they were mentally fast on their feet.

The following evening the two guys showed up at my hotel about seven o'clock. We went down to the parking lot, where they had a Rolls Royce waiting with a driver. We headed out of Kuwait City for about twenty-five minutes, and then, like the last time I went to meet a mullah, we slowed down and made a ninety-degree turn into the desert. It was just about sundown, and it started to get dark as we slowed down and stopped.

We got out and I saw a number of tents from the flashlights. I was also surprised to see other cars.

We were greeted by the mullah and led into a large tent where we sat on pillows. There were probably twenty-five men inside. Many had weapons. Tea was served along with some appetizers. Unfortunately, there were eyeballs, which I'd had previously. They tasted like the chicken cartilage between the drumstick and thigh. I had one to appease my host. Yum!

Then, to my surprise, three people appeared with instruments and started to play while a belly dancer performed. About fifteen minutes later, she stopped, and food was served. No utensils. The food was okay, but at that point there had been no business talk. Most of the talking had been in Arabic with virtually none directed at me.

I just smiled a lot.

After dinner, one of my entourage whispered in my ear that it was show time. I was to make the presentation to the mullah and that he would translate. The presentation was to buy a 150-acre vacant tract of commercial land in Houston that had utilities available for development. The price was a little less than $10 million, and it would take an additional $15–18 million in development costs. The presentation took fifteen minutes or so with no questions.

When I was through, there was a lot of discussion in Arabic between about half a dozen men. This discussion went on for probably another fifteen to twenty minutes, with no one asking me anything.

The next thing I knew, one of the men I came with said to shake hands and say, "*Assalamu alaikum*," a traditional Muslim greeting which means *peace to you*. I did as I was told and I left with one of the guys I'd come with. One of them stayed behind.

The gentleman who had bumped into me knocked on my hotel room door at 7:30 a.m. the next day. I let him in and said I had done what he wanted, but that I never wanted to see or hear from him again—in Kuwait or Houston. He understood, thanked me, and left.

Mahmoud never mentioned anything about this to me, taking whatever information he had to his grave.

8

IRAQ TRIP: THE ROAD TO BASRA

I'D BEEN STUCK in a lot of uncomfortable positions with Arabs before, but when I was stuck on that bus to Basra, Iraq surrounded by armed guerillas with my butt-cheeks clenched in fear, it was pretty hard to compare my situation with the previous experiences I'd had in Kuwait. Oh, some of them were wild too, but never this scary.

However, when the bus finally started moving, it created some ventilation. Fresh air quenched the flames of fear, and before too long, I was back to my problem-solving state of mind. I studied everything we drove past, thinking *We could build a subdivision here, a factory over there,* or *This would make a great retail site.* Because of the bombed-out bridges and bombed-out segments of road, there were a lot of detours and changes of direction.

Occasionally the bus would stop, and people got off. I was finally beginning to feel comfortable again. We continued driving along. Eventually, I turned away from sight-seeing long enough to suddenly notice I was the only person left on the bus. That was curious, given my impression that all the passengers were going to Basra. The bus continued traveling through a prairie area with no signs of life until it came to a crossroads. The driver slammed on the brakes, pulled over to the side of the road, and opened the door. He motioned for me to get out!

I shook my head *no.*

He motioned again for me to exit the bus.

I shook my head.

He then said something harsh in Arabic like, "Get off my fricking bus, you son of a motherless goat!"

I shook my head again.

The bus driver grabbed me by the arm and dragged me to the front door exit where he unceremoniously assisted me off the bus. He closed the doors and hauled ass.

I stood in the heat at the intersection of two roads somewhere in Iraq. I had no idea where I was, where Basra was, or where Kuwait was, and I saw no signs of human or animal life of any kind in any direction as far as I could see, not even a doghouse.

My ass was now solid steel. *Mission Control, I have a problem!*

How did I get myself into the absolute middle of nowhere in Iraq?

Time to go from a non-existent Plan B to Plan C . . . but I didn't have one of those either.

I stood there for about five minutes trying to decide which way to start walking. It was about noon, with the sun directly overhead and no shadows to tell me which way was north, south, east, or west.

Suddenly, out of nowhere, a bus like the one I was just booted off of appeared. It pulled over and stopped, and the bus driver opened the door.

I said, "Basra?"

The driver nodded.

"How much?"

"One Kuwaiti dinar."

I paid the man and got on hoping that this bus driver would take me where I wanted to go or at least point me in the right direction.

And, yeah. You guessed it; everyone on the bus appeared to be armed except me. I didn't care. *I'm saved,* I thought. *I might get to Basra yet.*

As I looked around at the dozen men on the bus, I noticed I was in better shape than last time—one of the men was unarmed. I assumed he'd forgotten to bring along his weapon that day.

As we entered an urban area, the bus driver asked me in perfect English, "Where do you want to go in Basra?"

I couldn't believe it. I'd made it! Or at least I hoped so. I told him the name of the hotel. About ten minutes later we pulled up in front of a small hill with a large building on top, and the bus driver motioned for me to get out. "This is your destination."

The entrance to the hotel had a big, circular drive that curved upward to an elevation about twenty feet above ground. I started walking up the drive. Just before I reached the entrance, a guy came out wearing cowboy boots and a cowboy hat.

He said, "Howdy."

I replied, "Howdy!" At that moment, I knew I was really saved!

Since I'd had such a harrowing trip, I thought I'd get something to eat and drink before I went to find my English-speaking limo driver to take me on a tour through Basra. I passed through the lobby into the air-conditioned restaurant.

A number of the tables held quart-sized bottles that I assumed were filled with water. The waiter who came to serve me spoke little English, but because of my previous trips to the Middle East, I was able to identify certain foods on the Arabic menu. I ordered one of the quart-sized bottles and a lamb dish, not knowing if it was baked or broiled. The waiter opened the bottle and poured it into a glass. It was carbonated and sure as hell looked like beer. Unbelievable. I tasted the golden liquid in my glass. It actually *was* beer!

I immediately ordered another one before the waiter could get away.

So there I was, in a Muslim country that I thought didn't allow liquor, and I was openly drinking a beer. If it had happened in Kuwait, I'd be lucky to be deported—if not jailed for a few years. Their rules had no limits. On the day I arrived in Kuwait City on my first trip to Kuwait, the Kuwaiti Court had sentenced a couple to a year in jail for kissing in public! Anyway, alcohol was forbidden publicly in Kuwait, but behind closed doors anything goes. It was common for a Kuwaiti host to ask me what alcohol I wanted to drink and then ask what brand. Usually, they had that brand in stock!

To find alcohol being served in an Iraqi restaurant was a pleasant shock, particularly after the trying morning I had just experienced.

The restaurant was very club-like with white tablecloths, wooden paneling, wooden floors arranged in a geometric pattern, and furnishings much like you would find in an American hotel. About ten to twelve other guests were eating in the restaurant, only one of them female. She was wearing a hijab and an expensive-looking long silk dress at the table next to mine with three men.

The nicest thing about the restaurant? None of the men appeared to carry rifles! They probably carried hidden pistols or had checked their weapons at the door, but at that point, I didn't care. I was enjoying my beer.

I went into the bathroom to freshen up before my meal came. I washed my hands and face, which were dusty as hell. The water was surprisingly cold and felt exhilarating—or was it the taste of the first beer getting to me? Either way, it was nice until I thought about the green, purple, and brown open sewage I had seen at the apartments. I resolved right there that in the future I would probably use bottled water to freshen up.

The food came, and the lamb was delicious. As I ate my meal, I chuckled to myself, given the events earlier in the day. If I died, I probably wouldn't have ordered a lamb dish as my last meal, but that I'd remember the experiences of that morning forever.

After a refreshing lunch, it was time to find my English-speaking limo driver. I asked at the front desk, "Where do I need to go to get my limo?"

The front-desk person said, "Go down to the end of that hall on your left."

Eager to begin my Basra tour, I bounced down the hall toward the car rental office. It looked more like the inside of a thatched-roof hut than a business. I said, "I'm here to get my limo."

Blank stare.

I asked for my limo again.

The blank stare continued.

I then told the man behind the counter my name and that I had reserved a limo.

There was absolutely no response. So, I said, "Mahmoud Al Adasani."

It was unbelievable. The guy behind the counter snapped to attention. Then he shook his head up and down and said, "Passport."

I handed him my passport.

After a quick check, he told me in broken English, "Sign this form for the car."

The form was in Arabic. I asked if he had a form in English.

He gave me a blank stare.

I asked again.

He shrugged and pointed for me to sign. So I signed. He then yelled a few words in Arabic to someone in a room behind the counter.

A guy came out who absolutely had to be the poster

boy for all terrorists if there ever was one! The thin, swarthy man had a five-day growth of stubble, disheveled hair, and beady eyes with a tic that jerked every few minutes. He said to me, "*Assalamu alaikum.*"

I said, "*Wa alaikum salaam.* Do you speak English?"

There was a blank stare. (So far, the people I had met on my trip to Iraq had really mastered the blank stare—they had it down to an art form.)

I asked again, "Do you speak English?"

No response.

Counter Guy said, "English no good."

Excruciatingly obvious, Sherlock. I then asked Poster Boy, "What is your name?"

Blank stare.

So I asked Counter Guy, "Do you have another driver who speaks better English?"

He shook his head and nodded toward Poster Boy. He addressed him with what I guess was a name—one I didn't quite catch—and then, in broken English, said, "Best driver."

I asked, "Do you have any other drivers who speak better English?"

Counter Guy shook his head again.

I sighed.

Then Counter Guy said something in Arabic to Poster

Boy, who started walking toward the exit. He stopped at the door and motioned for me to follow him. So I followed him outside expecting to find a newer shiny limo in the parking lot. But the so-called parking lot looked more like a used car lot for twenty- to thirty-year-old vehicles. The limo turned out to be a beaten-up gray panel truck that looked like it was left over from World War II! At least the tires seemed in good shape, like they were recently replaced.

What could possibly go wrong on this trip?

Anything and everything. I was in Iraq!

So I went back inside to the counter with Poster Boy trailing me. "Where is my limo?" I asked.

"Unfortunate accident." At least that's what I thought Counter Guy said.

"What kind of accident?"

Counter Guy made a strange motion with his hands, holding them together around his waist and then slowly moving them upward, separated over each shoulder.

This time I was the one with the blank stare.

He did it again.

No response from me.

Finally, in perfect English, he said, "Limo ran over mine."

I was flabbergasted! Given what had already transpired,

I shouldn't have been surprised. I didn't know if I should laugh or cry. I was afraid to ask the next question because I already knew the answer. "Do you have any other limos?"

"No."

"Do you have any other cars?"

"No."

"Are there any other limo companies that rent limos in Basra?"

"No."

I threw my hands up, stepped back out the door, and headed for the panel truck with Poster Boy trailing me. I came to Iraq to do a job, and I wasn't planning on leaving until I had answered most of my questions about the housing market and the potential for building a modular home factory in Basra. I was going to do whatever it took.

I opened the truck door. The inside was in even worse shape than the outside.

Looking at Poster Boy, I pointed to spot on the floor where the passenger seat was supposed to be. He reached into the back and plucked out what looked like an old apple crate and put it down. He motioned for me to sit on it.

I shook my head.

He reached in back again and drew out an old, ragged, oily blanket which he put over the crate, and motioned for me to get in. We were now ready to go—my limo, my English-speaking driver, and me.

After I settled my butt on the disgusting seat, I pointed to Poster Boy and made a circular motion with my finger, indicating, "Let's go."

He turned the key, but the engine didn't start. It didn't start the second time either. On the third try, the engine finally sputtered to life but it didn't sound like it was running on all cylinders. Instead of putting the truck into gear, Poster Boy let the engine idle for a couple of minutes. Although the engine started running more evenly as the truck warmed up, it sure seemed like it hadn't been running since World War II. But that was pretty much like everything else I'd seen so far in Iraq—from plastic ballpoint pens to second-hand-looking plastic sandals so worn that a thrift store would throw them away.

Suddenly, Poster Boy slammed the truck into drive and the air exploded with the sound of grinding gears.

So I'm sitting in an ancient truck with an Arabic terrorist-poster-boy driver who doesn't speak a lick of English, looks like he would slit my throat in a heartbeat, and doesn't know how to drive a stick shift!

Yeah, what could go wrong?

I just hoped he remembered where he had planted all the land mines!

9

SUSPECT BY ASSOCIATION

THE AMERICAN GOVERNMENT always assumed the Arabs were up to no good when we did business with them. That put us in a lot of uncomfortable situations and had us feeling as though we were being watched by Big Brother. But the thing is, the Arabs were never sneaky or conniving like the government thought. They were completely honest and straight forward with everything—even when, sometimes, their ideas didn't quite jive with American laws.

LOOKING FOR ARMAMENT

The whole time that Iraq and Iran were at war, we had people coming into our offices constantly to try and buy weapons, armament, and everything in between. I really wish that we had been able to videotape some of those exchanges, which were unbelievable. The guys coming to our office sold to both sides, and I would guess that over a two-year period we got at least two to four in-person requests a month in in addition to numerous telephone calls. We were not interested in getting into the weapons business. Following are some examples of the requests we received:

A well-dressed gentleman came to my office and said Ahmed Al Babtain had recommended me to him. He opened his thin briefcase and showed me a spec sheet for a Bell Helicopter main rotor blade. I don't remember which model or the part number. I *do* remember that he told me the US list price. I think at the time they were about $8,500 a blade FOB (freight on board) to Dallas, but I could be wrong. He said he had a client who would buy three hundred of those main rotor blades at three times list price FOB to any port in Europe. With freight, it probably represented a $4 million to $4.5 million profit. They would put up a letter of credit for the total sales price from any major European bank on the front end, subject to inspection of the merchandise by the banker upon delivery. This was probably the most straightforward deal we were offered. No sale.

A gentleman met with my partner and me about a new weapon that they wanted us to market. This weapon would fire eight hundred grenades a minute. The problem was that the weapon needed to be fired from a stationary position where you could store mountains of grenades that took up space and weighed a lot. He actually had a film showing the invention in action. In five minutes of action the weapon fired four thousand grenades. No sale.

People always came in looking to buy newer military rifles and automatic weapons. One guy offered to buy five hundred 30-caliber machine guns as the first order and would take up to twenty-five hundred more. No sale.

One person wanted to buy rocket-propelled grenades in any quantity. No sale.

Another guy wanted to buy four PT (patrol torpedo) boats. No sale.

One guy came with a small suitcase of cash as a down payment for the weapons he wanted to buy. No sale.

Another person wanted to buy some Boeing 707s converted into cargo planes. This was almost of interest until he started talking about re-equipping the planes with weapons. No sale.

We told all these people, and more, that we didn't deal in weapons and the door was right over there.

BUYING A LIMO

Back in the early days, after we had closed one real

estate deal with Ahmed and he had a house under contract, he turned to Bill and me for help in a lot of areas. About a week after he signed the contract to buy Mel Powers's house, he came into our office and said, "I need some help buying a limo."

Holy guacamole, you can be assured that my partner and I had never gone limo shopping before. The first thing we needed to do was determine who sold limos in Houston. After we found a dealership that sold Continental limos, we set up an appointment to go look the next day. In the interim, we tried to do some research on limos, but this was prior to computers and a little trickier. Unfortunately, the next day came too soon for us. We wanted to be able to ask some semblance of intelligent questions. Instead it was resort to Plan B: we needed to dazzle Ahmed with our BS.

As it turned out, I had an emergency meeting and couldn't go. Bill picked up Ahmed and went to the dealership. The sales manager greeted Bill and Ahmed, and instead of passing them off to a salesman, he stayed with them. I guess it's true that sharks can smell the blood in the water from miles away.

The sales manager had obviously done his homework and thought he had a live one. He had done a better job of prequalifying Ahmed than we had. All we knew was that he was supposed to have money and he had closed a real estate deal with us. We were happy. We were thinking we might be able to do a few more deals with him if we were lucky.

The sales manager started to show Ahmed a top-of-the-line limo. The first question the sales manager asked was, "Do you want bulletproof glass with the extra metal plating for the passenger and motor compartments?"

Bill was in shock. This was so far off his radar screen. If he said anything, he would probably be putting his foot in his mouth. As it turned out, Ahmed was extremely knowledgeable about cars. We later found out that the Al Babtain family owned more car dealerships in the Middle East than any other company or family. I think the only thing my partner recommended was that Ahmed consider getting a white limo because white would reflect the heat during the summer better than the other colors. Ultimately, Ahmed did decide to go with a white one.

Initially, when we set up the appointment at the dealership, we thought this was a preliminary exploratory visit to look and ask a few questions.

Wrong!

Ahmed said he had decided, so they went into the manager's office and the manager drew up the contract.

Ahmed looked at the contract and said, "It is incorrect."

The sales manager asked what was wrong, and Ahmed said he wanted to buy two limos. My partner was stunned. I think Ahmed got a $5,000 discount on the second one. The sales manager then asked how he planned to pay for the limos. Ahmed proceeded to hand the sales manager a shiny credit card!

"How much do you want to pay down?"

"The whole thing."

We're talking over a hundred grand to be charged to a credit card in the early 1980s. I didn't know credit cards that big existed. The sales manager left to run a credit check. It wasn't five minutes when he returned and asked, "Ahmed, when do you want the limos delivered?"

He wanted one delivered that week and the other in a couple of weeks, since they needed to make some modifications to the second one. Ahmed and Bill then left—with Bill's head spinning. He couldn't believe what had actually happened.

When Bill and Ahmed got back in the car, Bill asked Ahmed, "Why did you need to buy two limos?"

He replied that one was for himself when he was in Houston and the second one was for guests who might be visiting.

Absolutely amazing!

MACHINE GUNS AND LIMOS

During our second year of doing business with the Arabs, Abdul (pseudonym), the son of another wealthy family from Saudi Arabia, was meeting at our office for business purposes. He was staying at Ahmed Al Babtain's house in Clear Lake. I needed to go check something out at Ahmed's house, so I decided to get a ride in Ahmed's limo to do the quick check, since the limo needed to come back to our offices after dropping off Abdul anyway.

Abdul and I got into the back of the limo for the forty-five-minute ride to Ahmed's house. About five minutes into our trip, Abdul reached down and folded back the prayer rug that was on the floor. Suddenly, I was looking at a fully automatic machine gun lying on the floor.

Abdul reached down, picked up the machine gun, and chambered a round. Hard to believe what I had just seen, but it was true.

I asked, "What's the heavy armament for?"

Abdul replied, "Just in case we run into any trouble."

Hell! Am I riding with a terrorist? Is he a nutcase? Are people pissed off at him? Are we going to be attacked by terrorists? I realized I was slowly sinking down in the seat so I wouldn't be so visible. I tried to sound matter of fact as I asked, "Do you carry a machine gun often?"

"All the time. You can never be too careful. Here, do

you want to look at it?"

"No thanks."

I decided right there, on the spot, that if I lived through the trip to Ahmed's house, I was never going to ride in the limo with Abdul again! Every time the limo slowed down, I braced myself for an ominous, pending attack. The trip felt like it lasted forever. That day must have been my lucky day because, although I was very uncomfortable on the trip, we made it there in one piece.

It seemed there was a new surprise or experience every time we dealt with the Arabs. Some were scary, some were not, but they were all new experiences and it was never dull.

NURSERYMAN'S LICENSE

The government kept their eyes on the green—and I'm not just talking about money. In the early 1980s, I decided I needed a nurseryman's license so I could buy plants and trees wholesale for our land development activities in Houston. Actually, Mahmoud told me to go get one, so I got an application, filled it out, and sent it in, not thinking anything about it.

A couple of weeks later, the receptionist buzzed me to say there were two gentlemen who wanted to see me about my nurseryman's license application. You need to remember that almost all our employees were eighteen to twenty-five years old, and with the exception of my partner and me, and all the employees dressed casually. The next thing I know two gentlemen appeared in my office wearing dark suits with thin ties, sporting crew cuts and dark sunglasses. They definitely didn't look like anybody I had ever met from the Texas Department of Agriculture, before or since.

I asked what was up. One of them tried to convince me that this was the normal review process for a nurseryman's license. I thought, *Yeah, I believe that!*

They started by asking what I thought were normal questions, like "Why do you want a nurseryman's license?" "How much product do you plan to buy yearly?" and questions about my locations. Then, after about ten minutes, came the corker.

"We understand that you are doing a lot of business out of the Middle East."

How in the world would the Texas Department of Agriculture know I'm doing business in the Middle East, and why would they care?

I answered, "Yes, we do business out of the Middle East."

Although they asked lots of questions about the Middle East, they didn't blatantly ask about any specific people we were dealing with. After half an hour or so, they left. This really was a very strange meeting.

My nurseryman's license arrived in the mail a couple of weeks later. To this day I have no idea what agency they worked for, but you can bet your sweet patootie it wasn't the Texas Department of Agriculture!

SPOOKS

My nurseryman license application wasn't the only time I encountered agency people. After every trip my partner or I made to the Middle East, a number of spooks would line up at our doorstep, either individually or in pairs. They stood out like sore thumbs in our office full of young employees in casual attire.

Even now I don't know for sure what agencies or governments they represented. But if I were a spy working for the CIA, I probably wouldn't hand someone a card saying I worked for the CIA. All the people were well groomed except the guy who said he was from the Israeli Mossad. He was a large, overweight slob with unusually thick glasses and disheveled hair who acted like a complete clod. Maybe he was Mossad, maybe he wasn't. I'll never know.

From the questions that were asked, I lost all faith in the US State Department—if that's really where they were from. Those guys wouldn't know which way was out if you showed them the door. Some of the State Department people asked seriously dumb questions. They would ask about recent trips where we had seen someone for thirty minutes or less and expect us to answer very detailed questions.

One time a guy was grilling me about a short meeting I had had in Kuwait. Funny thing is, the Kuwaiti they were talking about had been in our Houston offices for a whole week two weeks before I had gone on that trip to Kuwait. I assumed the guy asking the questions was clueless about this person's trip to Houston.

In a lot of cases, they wanted to know if we were aware if a particular person met with another particular person. There were questions about dress, girlfriends, eating habits, drinking habits, playing around, work habits, and so on. Occasionally they would show us a picture and ask if we had seen that person. We complied in any way we could.

10

RISKY BUSINESS

OUR INTERACTIONS WITH the Arabs may have looked like risky business to the American government, but the real risky business about dealing with the Arabs may have been more about playtime than business. They have a strong attraction to jet setting, pretty girls, and Las Vegas.

Most Kuwaitis were horrible gamblers, with the exception of the professional gamblers who came in from the Middle East. When they went to Las Vegas it was almost as if they were buying entertainment, and losing was the cost of admission. Obviously, the reason the casinos sucked up to the Kuwaitis so much was because they were terrible gamblers who typically lost a lot of money.

Over time, my partner and I learned that most of the Kuwaitis we dealt with were speculators and opportunists in business. Not all, but most. They liked the long-shot home runs. These guys typically weren't looking for the steady 8–10 percent returns on their investments. They wanted quick action.

In Kuwait, it was normal to see these guys in their offices looking at video screens showing real-time currency exchange rates. A lot of them were very actively buying and selling currencies, stock options, commodities, and so on. They liked the excitement of fast-moving markets where they were in and out quickly. They were traders who speculated daily.

I can't tell you how many times I watched one of the Kuwaitis lose $100,000 within an hour at a Las Vegas blackjack, craps, or baccarat table. Typically, they didn't play the slot machines, and seldom were they at the roulette table—with the exception of Mahmoud. A few played poker, especially the professional gamblers, and some of the hybrid card games. Not all but most were good tippers which didn't hurt; the hotel staff sucked up.

Most of the time, the Kuwaitis preferred to play on the main floor at the regular casino as opposed to the high-roller areas, which were usually quieter and more subdued. I think they liked to show off their wealth to the general public, although there was almost always less to show off when they left the casinos!

PASSPORTS AND STRIP CLUBS

The Kuwaitis we dealt with typically flew directly from Kuwait to London, with a few days' layover in London, and then from London to New York with a layover of a few days in New York. After that it was another nonstop from New York to Las Vegas, with a long layover of several days to a couple of months. Then they either flew directly back to Kuwait or had a layover in Houston along the way.

The Kuwaitis consistently invited us to fly out to Las Vegas to meet with them for a few days, which got old quickly. In many cases, we were able to get them to come to Houston after they got bored in Las Vegas. A number of these Kuwaitis owned or had access to private jets but preferred to fly commercially on longer flights.

Almost everyone we dealt with traveled on a diplomatic passport. In fact, we began to think that the government of Kuwait issued *only* diplomatic passports because it seemed like everyone had one. They rarely seemed to help Kuwaitis in the US unless they were checking into the hotels at the casinos in Las Vegas, where they always got big suites. In reality, that could have been a result of their poor gambling history and the hotels' way to keep them coming anyway. I never knew.

On a couple of occasions, the diplomatic passports

actually did help. One of those took place at Caligula's and one at Rick's Cabaret, the Arab strip club of choice.

Caligula's was your typical strip club with thirty to forty waitresses/dancers, but there was one major exception: every half hour or so a certain song would come on. When it did all the girls throughout the place would stop what they were doing and start bumping and grinding on the spot.

As luck would have it, the first time we took Ahmed to Caligula's, we sat down just as the song started playing. There were two girls adjacent to our table and a third probably ten feet away. Ahmed eyes widened like saucers as he watched. Needless to say, Ahmed returned to Caligula's many times.

Taking Arabs who were traveling on diplomatic passports with ungodly amounts of money to strip clubs presented major problems. The Arabs were accustomed to getting whatever they wanted when they wanted it. The problem was that the girls were very attractive and sexually provocative, but the patrons weren't supposed to touch the girls. We had more than one close encounter where a bouncer was ready to do bodily harm to one of our clients. The first time it happened was with a very good client who had grabbed one of the girls and sat her in his lap.

The next thing I knew, some guy who looked like the Incredible Hulk showed up out of nowhere. He had to be a head taller than me and weighed a hundred pounds more—and the extra weight looked like it was all muscle. Before I realized what I was doing, I jumped up to get between the menacing bouncer and our client.

I said, "There's been a friendly misunderstanding. These gentlemen are from Kuwait and weren't familiar with the house rules." I instantly thought, *You know that excuse sounds pretty lame.*

The bouncer must have thought the same thing because he said, " I don't give a frick if they're from Mars because I'm going to beat the ever-living dog crap out of this guy."

"You can't do that. This client is a billionaire traveling on a diplomatic passport."

The bouncer growled, "Yeah, yeah, I believe that. Get out of my way." He took a step closer until his body and mine were actually touching.

"Stop! Would you please go get the manager and I'll explain it to him?"

Incredibly, he thought about it for ten seconds or so, all the while with a menacing stare, and then told one of the girls to go get the manager. He was obviously thinking it was a long shot but I might be telling the truth.

It was a very tense minute or so before the manager came to our table. I explained the situation. I didn't think he nor the City of Houston wanted a diplomatic incident; they surely wouldn't want the possibility of negative publicity.

The manager asked, "Can I see your diplomatic passports?" and two were produced.

The manager then turned to the Incredible Hulk and said, "It's okay. I'll handle it from here."

Grateful and relieved, I said, "I'm really sorry about this. It won't happen again."

I was thinking that it really *wouldn't* ever happen again. Little did I know it was going to happen another half dozen times or so in the future! Sometimes dealing with extremely wealthy Arabs presented unexpected issues.

FAROUK'S DATE

Farouk (pseudonym), the son of one of the wealthiest families in the whole Middle East, was doing a real estate deal with us. This man was in his mid-twenties, handsome, and very well spoken. He obviously went to the best schools and colleges. He was sort of nerdy, but very personable. Since he was going to be in town for the night, I asked him if he would like to go out for dinner and a few drinks. It sounded like fun to him.

Almost all the guys from the Middle East liked good steak, so I picked him up at seven o'clock, and we went to Brenner's Steakhouse on the Katy Freeway. Brenner's is owned by a German family. It's an old-line steakhouse with excellent steaks and a good wine list. I thought we could have dinner and I might spend a hundred dollars with tip.

I looked over the wine list to pick out a good red wine to go with the steaks. I decided we ought to have a 1961 Troplong Mondot, one of my favorite French Bordeaux wines at the time from an outstanding year. It was a little pricey, but what the heck, this was not a wine readily available and it was $125 a bottle.

Farouk asked if he could see the wine list. The next thing I knew he had changed the order to a $475 bottle of 1961 Chateaux La Tour, a very famous first-growth Bordeaux. It was an outstanding, robust red wine with a very long finish. When the wine steward brought the bottle to our table, Farouk made a big deal out of tasting the wine and then told the wine steward that it was excellent. Oh, really? At $475 a bottle, which I'm paying for, I would hope it's good!

By the time we had eaten our salads with blue-cheese dressing, we had finished off the first bottle, and Farouk ordered another. My plans for an economical evening had just gone down the toilet. I figured at this rate I'd have to go to the bank the next day to try to pay for the bar bill, and we hadn't even gone to a strip club yet. Luckily, we slowed down on the second bottle. The rib eyes were excellent. We had dessert and finished off the second bottle of wine.

When the bill came, we argued over who would pay the bill. I wanted to pay it (not really) and he wanted to pay it. So I let him win the argument.

Then Farouk said, "Let's go meet some girls."

We went over to Caligula's, the strip club favored by many of our clients, located just north of Westheimer Road about a mile west of the Galleria. As we walked into Caligula's, they started playing that song. All the girls throughout the club stopped what they were doing and started bumping and grinding. To say Farouk's eyes got as big as platters would have to be an absolute understatement. He was in complete shock. Obviously, he had never been to a strip club like this. After the girls stopped, we ordered drinks.

Farouk asked, "Is that normal?"

I replied, "Yes."

He couldn't believe it. "There are so many good-looking women. Are all these women available?"

I said, "Probably most."

Farouk immediately took a liking to a small, very attractive brunette. As the evening progressed, I excused myself to go to the bathroom. As I headed that way, I ran into the brunette.

I asked her if she wanted a date that night after she got off work.

She said, "I might, but it'll cost you $500 for an hour."

She was expensive, but if it made Farouk happy, I'd be happy. And Farouk did pay for dinner.

I said, "Okay." I wrote down Farouk's name, hotel, and room number. I then handed her $500 in cash. This was not normal, but I'd had a lot to drink and I thought, What the hell?

I told her, "Go to that room around 1:30 a.m."

I went back to the table and was surprised that Farouk didn't say anything about how long I was gone. It was obvious: Farouk was having a good time.

We finally stumbled out of the club about 1:00 a.m. I dropped Farouk off about fifteen minutes later and told him I would see him in my office tomorrow at 3:00 p.m. I assumed that Farouk was getting ready to have a great time.

The next afternoon Farouk came to the office all bright-eyed and bushy-tailed, looking like he's had a wonderful time. We talked about business for about half an hour.

Then he said, "I want to tell you about last night. I had a really great time at the steakhouse and Caligula's. About fifteen minutes after I got back to my room, there was a knock on the door. When I opened the door, I was shocked to see the cute brunette from the club."

Farouk let her in, and she asked what he wanted to do.

She asked if he wanted to get in bed, or did he have something else in mind? He was in complete shock. He was tired and suggested she go home. That's when she told him I had paid for her. Farouk again was shocked. Finally, she asked if she could at least stay in his room for a half hour before she left. So they talked for a while and she left.

Farouk said, "I wanted to thank you for your generosity, but it was not necessary." He told me he might see her on his next trip to Houston.

Even though it didn't work out the way I had anticipated, Farouk was happy, so I was happy.

EXPENSIVE SUITE

One fine Thursday in 1983, Mahmoud called me from Las Vegas and said he wanted to see me there. I told him I didn't need a fancy room and that I would need to be back in Houston Sunday night. So I flew out the next day to meet him.

I checked in at the front desk at Caesar's Palace and went to my room. It was a nice room with a king bed and a jetted tub in the bathroom. As I was putting my stuff up, I noticed a door and decided to open it.

Holy crap!

You would not believe what I saw.

A white grand piano on a raised pedestal; a poker table with seating for eight; a stocked bar with four barstools; a dining room that seated ten people; a movie-viewing area; three sitting areas, one of which would probably have seated a dozen people; and a small reading area with bookshelves and books.

I'm in pretty good shape, and I can tell you that I probably couldn't have thrown a football from one end of the room to the other. It was that big.

When I saw Mahmoud, I asked him, "What's up with the room?"

He replied, "I thought you needed to unwind."

I could have unwound with my closest hundred friends in that room. Mahmoud had a generous interpretation of simplicity.

BIG GREEN IDEAS

I don't know how many of you have been to Las Vegas,

but those who have will say grass is something you don't see a lot of. Remember, Las Vegas is in the dessert.

Mahmoud called me from Las Vegas and said he wanted me to come out for a few days. As was typical, I dropped everything and immediately went to him.

I checked in at the front desk of Caesar's Palace, one of the hotels preferred by people from the Middle East, although we occasionally stayed at the Desert Inn, Circus, and some other forgettable hotel. The desk clerk gave me a note from Mahmoud. It said he wanted to see me immediately. I was thinking, *He probably wants to talk to me about some big real estate deal in Houston.*

I went to my room to freshen up before meeting him. I then called the front desk to ask which suite Mahmoud was in. The clerk said Mahmoud was in 111A—or some similar number—which suggested his suite was on the ground floor. That didn't make any sense to me. All the suites I had seen previously were on the top floors, and they had four numbers, with the first two digits representing the floor number and the last two, the room number. Mahmoud wouldn't stay on the ground floor.

So I went downstairs to the front desk to try to straighten out the problem. I approached the front desk and asked, "What suite is Mahmoud Al Adasani in?"

The desk clerk replied, "One eleven A."

I asked, "What floor is that on?"

"The first floor."

I said, "I thought all your nice suites are on the top floors of the hotel."

"Most are, but there is one special suite on the first floor."

"Oh. Where is it located?"

"Go down the hall to the left, out the door, through the breezeway to one eleven A."

I said thanks, and headed down the hall.

As soon as I opened the door to the breezeway, the temperature went up forty degrees. It literally took my breath away. I walked down the breezeway to a freestanding building that said 111A on the door. I knocked.

Mahmoud answered the door and said, "Welcome to my humble abode."

As I walked inside, I couldn't believe what I was seeing. Most of the exterior walls had floor-to-ceiling glass overlooking a private walled patio with a private swimming pool and grass. There was probably more grass than I had in my yard at my home in Houston. I think it also had a private putting green. The entire suite was at least eighteen hundred square feet. Never before—or since—have I seen a Las Vegas hotel or casino room with a fully grassed yard. It was unbelievable.

About that time, a really gorgeous nymph came out of the bedroom and said, "Hi, I'm going to take a swim."

And she was out the door.

Mahmoud asked, "What do you think?"

I said, "It is unbelievable." Of course, I was talking about the girl, not the suite.

Mahmoud said, "I rented it for the next six weeks."

I said, "The girl?"

He said, "No, no, the suite. What do you think?"

I told Mahmoud, "It is really exceptional. As is your taste in women."

He laughed and said he wanted to show me the suite because he had the idea of replicating it in Kuwait City and building fifty to one hundred units. "What do you think?"

"From a construction standpoint you could do it, but I have some major concerns."

"Like what?"

"Well, the first issue is the outside pool. It would probably need to be an indoor pool in Kuwait because of the high exterior heat and evaporation problems. Although they have these problems in Las Vegas, the cost of water is tremendously cheaper here than in Kuwait because in Kuwait all the fresh water comes from two major desalination plants. In turn, an indoor pool would be more expensive to build than an outdoor pool.

"Secondly, the walled area surrounding the compound would probably need to be twelve to sixteen feet high to block out morning and late-afternoon direct sun. The higher wall would result in more initial construction cost.

"Thirdly, grass would be very difficult to grow through the hottest part of the day. There may need to be some type of filtered screen ten to fifteen feet above the grass to keep it from burning up during the middle of the day. That is in addition to the major cost of watering and maintaining the grass in Kuwait.

"Fourth, you would probably need to put some type of reflective solar film over the floor-to-ceiling glass. In addition, the air-conditioning cost would be dramatically higher, both for the larger AC unit required plus the actual monthly operating cost to cool the unit."

Mahmoud thought for a minute and said, "Do you think it would be practical in Kuwait?"

I said, "Mahmoud, it is a neat idea and this place is beautiful, but you would lose your rear if you tried to replicate these units for sale in Kuwait."

Mahmoud then said, "Both the Kuwaitis who were here yesterday thought it would be a wonderful idea and that I could make a bunch of money."

"Were either of them in the construction business?"

Mahmoud replied, "No."

"Have either of them ever been involved directly as an owner building real estate projects?"

"No."

"Mahmoud, I would not recommend that you do this."

"That is why I invited you out here. I knew you would tell me the truth. Thank you. Now let's go have some fun in the casino."

We then went to gamble in the casino. I assumed the management at Caesar's Palace thought Mahmoud was going to lose a bunch of money, and Mahmoud did not disappoint them. I don't know for sure what this six-week trip to Las Vegas ultimately cost Mahmoud, but I would think it was in the low seven figures when the numbers were tallied up.

To Mahmoud, it was just entertainment.

AN (ALMOST) INTERNATIONAL INCIDENT

On another trip to Las Vegas that year, Mahmoud asked me to fly out and meet him for a few days. I checked into the typical over-the-top Caesar's Palace room. The room had two king-sized beds with a whirlpool bath and a large sitting area. I called Mahmoud as soon as I checked in, but he had left "Do not disturb" instructions at the front desk. So, what else? I went and gambled for a few hours. It was a nice and pleasant break. Afterward, I went up to the room for an hour's nap.

Mahmoud called around seven to say, "Meet me at the entrance in an hour for dinner."

I went down about ten minutes early and saw some of his party, including his personal relations guy—a bodyguard, I thought—named Sultan Murad. We greeted each other and made small talk while waiting for Mahmoud. Mahmoud came down ten minutes later and immediately said he felt lucky. He motioned for me to follow him to the baccarat table. He quickly asked for $20,000 in chips. About ten minutes later he said he was ready to go eat. Oh, by the way, Mahmoud had just won $275,000! He acted as casually as someone who had just gotten up from the blackjack table after winning $20. Dealing with the Arabs really was different.

Mahmoud wanted to go to some Middle Eastern restaurant that was supposed to have a fantastic belly dancer and Middle Eastern band. So we all piled into a limo for the ride over. There were seven of us in total: one of the guys was a professional gambler from the Gulf region, I think one was a relative of Mahmoud's, two were business associates, his bodyguard, Mahmoud, and me.

I don't remember the name of the restaurant where we

ate, but the food was Middle Eastern, and I sure as hell remember the belly dancer. She was a real dark-haired beauty, a gorgeous firecracker, and probably more dangerous. I don't think I have ever seen a more erotic performance with clothes on in my life. The restaurant had a three-person Middle Eastern band with a drummer, a keyboardist, and a guitar player.

We were sitting at a large, round table adjacent to the dance floor. As the band played, the hot belly dancer started her motor. It was unbelievable!

The two businessmen sitting on either side of me went wild. One of them yelled something in Arabic to the belly dancer. The music stopped, and she instantly ran over to our table, yelling at the businessman. I stood up to get between them and was probably two feet away from her, as well as from the businessman next to me, who had also gotten up.

To this day I don't know exactly what he said to the belly dancer, but there was no question that she didn't like it at all. I thought I had previously met some fast-talking women in Mexico. Wrong! This girl started screaming in Arabic so fast it sounded like a siren. She was wild-eyed, crazy looking. The only reason the guy she was yelling at wasn't scorched by her flames was that the other businessmen with us threw a drink on her!

It was as if an atom bomb had gone off, and I was just a foot away!

The next thing I knew, the bouncer and restaurant manager were at my side.

The manager said to the bouncer, "Arrest everyone."

I said, "What?" in disbelief.

"I want them all arrested," the manager said again.

I said, "You can't do that."

"Why not?"

I said, "Could I please talk to you in private for a minute? It is important."

The manager begrudgingly agreed, and we went to his office.

I told him that I was traveling with the undersecretary to the oil minister of Kuwait and that all the other people there, other than myself, were traveling on diplomatic passports. I didn't think that he wanted an international incident and all the possible negative publicity that might bring.

He scowled at me and asked, "Is Mahmoud really the undersecretary to the oil minister of Kuwait?"

So I went and got all their passports and brought them back to the manager. I also had some official-looking thing, like a fold-over wallet a detective would use in showing a badge, showing Mahmoud was the undersecretary.

The manager looked at all of them.

I then said, "How much money would it take to resolve the problem?" Without hesitation, he said, "Fifteen hundred dollars."

I reached in my pocket and counted out $1,500 in hundred-dollar bills (luckily, I had been winning at the blackjack tables).

He handed me back everyone's passports and Mahmoud's wallet and said, "Leave."

We were out of Dodge in a heartbeat.

Thank you, Lord. I thought I was going to spend the night bailing everyone out of the pokey if we survived the fight with the management—that was, if I wasn't arrested too. Just another normal evening with the Arabs.

JOHNNY CARSON'S JET

About a year later, in mid-August of 1984, I met with Mahmoud Al Adasani in Las Vegas. He had a whole entourage with him. I'm not sure how many of the people were traveling with him and how many he had just met in Las Vegas. There had to have been at least a dozen men with him. Sultan Murad, his friend and possible bodyguard, was there. I always liked Sultan and we got along very well. There were one or two professional gamblers, some business associates, and some what I'll call hangers-on, guys who were along for the free ride. I generally thought the hangers-on were mostly worthless people and never understood why they were there.

I went up to Mahmoud's suite, where five or six guys were bickering around the dining room table about what to order for a snack. Part of the discussion was in English, and the louder part was in Arabic. Finally, Mahmoud couldn't stand the arguing any longer; he called room service. He told them he wanted two large fruit platters and one of every appetizer they had.

Suddenly, silence filled the room.

I could not believe how quickly they got Mahmoud's order out. I'll bet it wasn't twenty minutes later when there was a knock at Mahmoud's door. It opened to ten waiters, maybe more, delivering the food. There was so much food that it completely covered the dining table—which seated twelve—the tables in the sitting area, the top of the bar, and I think they put two or three dishes on the bathroom countertops. There were probably twenty-five different appetizers not counting two large fruit platters! I will say this: Mahmoud was a big tipper and it showed. The casino personnel did a lot of serious sucking up to him.

After a couple of days, I was up $4,000 and getting bored. The 1984 Los Angeles Summer Olympics had just started. I was at a blackjack table, and Mahmoud came over and asked if I wanted to go to the Summer Olympics in Los Angeles.

I said, "Sure."

Mahmoud said, "See that pit boss over at the craps table?" I nodded.

He said, "Go tell him what you want to go see."

So I got up and went over to the craps table and asked to speak to the pit boss. I told him that we'd like to go to the Olympics.

He said, "When?"

I said, "How about tomorrow?"

He said, "Fine. What do you want to see?"

I didn't have a fricking clue. I was absolutely flabber-gasted that I might be going to the Olympics to begin with. I shrugged my shoulders.

He said he would get me a list of events with available tickets.

I wondered back over to the blackjack table in shock. As I was sitting there, a guy brought over a list. Now you need to understand that when I was growing up in Tex-as, if the waiter asked you if you wanted wine with din-ner, your choices were red, white, or rosé, meaning they only had one wine in each category. As I got older, when I went to a nice restaurant in New York and they asked if

I wanted wine, they would typically bring me a wine list two to six pages long.

The list for the Olympics looked like a large telephone book. Everything was in a loose-leaf binder, and the pages went on and on. There were so many events that I didn't recognize a few of them. On each event they had a list of available tickets. They had tickets to every event, but they were very limited for the Closing Ceremony.

The whole thing was really overwhelming. Going to the Olympics had not been on my radar screen that morning, and suddenly I had pick of the litter to any event I wanted to see. I finally decided we ought to go see the preliminary diving competition because I thought it would be neat to see Greg Louganis take the plunge.

Mahmoud came over and asked if I had decided.

I said, "How about the diving preliminaries tomorrow?"

Mahmoud asked, "Why?"

"I have always wanted to see Greg Louganis dive."

Mahmoud said, "I'll make arrangements for a group of us to fly to Los Angeles in Johnny Carson's private jet tomorrow morning."

"Are you serious?"

He said, "There are a few advantages to being the undersecretary to the oil minister of Kuwait."

Oh, really!

I decided to go for a walk outside, but it was hot as Hades in mid-August in Las Vegas. After about a minute, reason prevailed and I decided to wander around some of the shops.

Big mistake!

While wandering around I saw a women's backless, metallic-gold evening halter-top. It looked really neat on the mannequin, but I wondered how it would look on my wife. A young saleslady on the other side of the shop looked like my wife's size. Her breasts looked similar in size too, so I asked the woman I was working with if the other saleslady would model this top. If she did, I'd probably buy it.

My saleslady brought the other saleslady over to meet me. Up close this girl looked like a showgirl in her early twenties. She said she'd be happy to model the top and went over and put it on. When she came back, it was a knockout. The top was meant to be worn without a bra and was extremely slinky. Suddenly, there were a half dozen men milling around, admiring her endowment.

I said I would take it without realizing how expensive it was. It was an $1,800 top. I sure as heck hoped my wife liked it. (As it turned out, she never wore the damned thing. Not even once!)

The next morning, I met Mahmoud and four other Kuwaitis for the limo ride to the airport. And as Mahmoud had said, it really was Johnny Carson's private jet with his personal pilots. I had ridden in a number of private jets before, and I thought the jet was nothing special other than who owned it.

We sat in raised bleachers at the outdoor diving pool for the Olympics ten-meter platform-diving preliminaries. Actually, the seats were excellent. I don't know how many different divers we saw, but I would guess about one hundred fifty, and each diver made two dives. Other than Mahmoud, the Kuwaitis I was with were an embarrassment. They stomped their feet, whistled, and jumped up to yell in Arabic. Some of their words, I was told later by Mahmoud, were very unflattering.

The country of Kuwait had one diver at the Olympics, and he was among the worst, but the Kuwaitis carried on like they were rooting for the Super Bowl champs.

There were a number of excellent divers, but in my opinion, Greg Louganis performed the most flawless dives with virtually no splash on entry. It really was amazing watching him dive. After his performance, I was ready to leave because the guys in our group were acting like real schmucks, but Mahmoud wanted to stay. So I endured the insults the Kuwaitis screamed for another two hours. Finally, it was over.

We flew back to Las Vegas late that afternoon—on Johnny Carson's jet—and I took the first flight back to Houston the next morning. Luckily, I never saw those rude schmucks again. And luckily, the majority of the Arabs I dealt with were nothing like them.

CUTTING BACK IN LAS VEGAS

On one trip to Las Vegas, Mahmoud told me, "You know, I've been here in Las Vegas three weeks, and I need to cut back on my spending. Why don't we have Chinese food this evening?"

I said, "That sounds fine with me."

This was the only time I ever heard Mahmoud say he wanted Chinese food. He liked fine dining, good beef and lamb, French and Italian food.

We met at eight to have Chinese food at a restaurant in Caesar's Palace. We sat down and ordered a typical American assortment of dishes.

Then Mahmoud asked the waiter, "Could I please see your wine list?

The waiter brought back a very simple wine list with maybe three white wines.

Mahmoud said, "I would like a bottle of Le Montrachet."

The waiter said, "We don't have that wine."

Mahmoud said, "Send someone upstairs to your French restaurant and tell them Mahmoud Al Adasani wants two bottles of Le Montrachet."

About twenty minutes later the wine steward from the restaurant upstairs showed up with two cold bottles of Le Montrachet.

Mahmoud really did cut back on expenses that night at dinner. The Chinese food with tip was less than $40. On the other hand, the wine was over $2,000!

Another Arab moment.

TABLE FOR ONE

The next day, after that strange approach to cutting back, I ran into Mahmoud in the lobby. He wanted to play roulette and asked me to sit with him. So we went into the casino. It looked like half the casino was empty. There were two open roulette tables. The first one was packed, and the second one had about a dozen people playing at it.

Mahmoud said, "That isn't what I wanted."

The next thing I knew, Mahmoud was speaking to one of the pit bosses, and then he motioned for me to follow him.

Mahmoud sat down at one of the closed roulette tables, and a couple of minutes later, a crew showed up and roped off our table making it private. Then a croupier showed up with two guys trailing him carrying chips and money. In five minutes, Mahmoud was playing roulette by himself.

Mahmoud's bets varied from $1,000 to $25,000 a spin.

In all my years of gambling, I had never before sat at a gaming table opened up specifically for someone I was with. That was, until that day.

LOSS LIMITS

When I go to a casino, I normally set a loss limit of $5,000–10,000 before I go. If I lose that amount of money, I stop gambling for the remainder of the trip. Well, I had lost my limit, so I had stopped gambling.

Mahmoud asked me to join him at a roulette table. I did, but he noticed I wasn't gambling. He asked, "What's wrong? Why aren't you gambling?"

I told Mahmoud, "I lost all the money I wanted to lose this trip."

He said, "You know you came out here to have fun." With that he handed me ten $1,000 chips and said, "Go have a good time."

I was in a funky mood and didn't give a damn. I really didn't feel like gambling, so I thought I would go over to the baccarat table, where I would win or lose a bunch quickly. Six hands later I went back and sat down next to Mahmoud.

He asked, "How did you do?"

I said, "I won the first hand and lost the next five."

"Well, how did you do?"

"I lost it all."

Mahmoud then said, "You know, maybe you should take a break."

Really?

HIGH-ROLLER BABYSITTER'S CLUB

In 1985, Mahmoud called me to say he was in Las Vegas again and wanted me to join him the next day. So, as was typical in dealing with the Arabs, I canceled everything I was doing for the rest of the week and booked a flight to Las Vegas.

Normally at that period of my life, I wore jeans and a sports coat when I travelled, but because it was summer and hotter than hell in Las Vegas, I decided to wear jeans and a blue denim short-sleeved shirt. Unbeknownst to me, there was a tear in the back of the shirt. I also put on a pair of old, but comfortable beat-up cowboy boots. I seldom wore cowboy boots except when I was with people from overseas. It's what they expected to see in Texas, and I wanted to play the part.

Anyway, I got to the airport, and as I was entering the plane, a stewardess pointed out the rip in the back of my shirt. Terrific! I look like a ragamuffin, going to meet the undersecretary to the oil minister of Kuwait.

I sat down next to a guy in the oil business who had spent an unusually large amount of time in the Middle East. After he told me what he was doing, I told him I was going to Las Vegas to meet the undersecretary to the oil minister of Kuwait. Remember, I was wearing a torn denim short-sleeved shirt with old cowboy boots and jeans. I figured he thought I was blowing smoke up his rear.

We continued some light conversation all the way to Las Vegas. The plane landed, and as we taxied to the terminal, the captain made a special announcement over the intercom. "We have a very important guest on board. Would everyone please remain seated when the plane comes to a stop at the terminal? Mr. Koshkin, your limo driver is waiting for you."

When I got up to leave, you should have seen my seat mate's jaw drop. As I toddled down the aisle, I saw some priceless expressions. The limo driver was not waiting at the gate. He was at the plane's door when they opened the hatch!

The driver took me to Caesar's Palace, where Mahmoud had gotten me one of the smaller suites I had ever stayed in when the Arabs were hosting—a double suite with two king beds, a Jacuzzi, and a dining area. I called for Mahmoud, but he was taking a nap, so I went down and gambled for a few hours. Not a good idea. I lost about five grand.

Mahmoud came down about 6:15 p.m., and he had his nineteen-year-old son with him.

As we were eating at one of the casino restaurants, Mahmoud said he was bored, even though he'd only been there one day. He then said, "We're all going to Lake Tahoe tomorrow."

I nodded. What else was I going to do?

The next day we flew to Lake Tahoe and checked into one of the nice casino hotels. This was the first time I had ever been to Lake Tahoe. The room was the typical large suite, but it had a beautiful view for a change. I was accustomed to getting up early and walking for forty-five minutes or more three or four times a week, usually doing fourteen-and-a-half-minute miles. Compared to Las Vegas, Lake Tahoe was a breath of fresh air. The beautiful lake, trees, and mountains were a pleasant change from the desert landscape of Las Vegas.

Usually when I go to a casino, I set a limit of how much I am willing to lose or make. When I hit the loss or win amount, I shut it down for the rest of the trip. I had already lost $5,000 and a couple more after dinner in Las Vegas. The first afternoon in Lake Tahoe I lost another $3,000, which caused me to reach my loss limit of $10,000, so I stopped playing.

Mahmoud knew I played with limits and that I had lost all I wanted to lose, so while he and his son were playing blackjack, he asked me, "Ben, please watch my son and make sure he doesn't get into any trouble."

I said I would be happy to, while thinking, *Uh-oh! I'm in a ton of trouble now.*

His son was nineteen with raging hormones. He was very handsome, about six one and 180 pounds with a good athletic build. He spoke fluent English, Arabic, French, and some Spanish. Taking him to a casino was like taking a fox to a hen house for a three-day visit. All I could imagine was the carnage! The real question was, how *much* carnage? It really wasn't going to be pretty, and I was responsible.

I thought, *Boy, am I going to have fun this trip.*

The son immediately said he wanted to go to some shows, particularly Playboy's Playmates of Nevada.

I called the concierge and got tickets to see Playboy's Playmates of Nevada that evening and another show the next night at another casino. All afternoon, as I watched Mahmoud's son gamble, he would get a case of whiplash every time a good-looking female walked by. Unfortunately, he got more than his fair share of reciprocal smiles.

I thought, *This is not going to end well.*

That night, I met Mahmoud's son for a light dinner at the LA Italian Restaurant, and then we went to see Playboy's Playmates of Nevada. We sat at a table about fifteen feet from the stage. The curtains opened to show three gorgeous Playmates sitting on a motorcycle. At first, I thought they were totally nude, but after five minutes I realized they were wearing incredibly small flesh-colored G-strings. The first ten minutes were the second most erotic thing I've ever seen without actual sex, the first being the belly dancer in Las Vegas—the one some Arabs had almost launched an international incident over.

Mahmoud's son was going bonkers. He was in love. The lead blonde was going to be his wife and bear his children.

He said, "We must go backstage and meet her immediately."

I said, "No." I was actually thinking not *No*, but *Hell no, not a chance.*

The son wanted to send her a note. "Why can't I go backstage and meet her? How about some Swiss chocolate? How about roses?"

I thought, *Am I having fun yet?*

I needed to gag this guy and chain him to the table, although I'm not sure that chaining him to the table would have held him down.

He asked our cocktail waitress if she knew the lead blonde's name, and she said *no*. Before I could do anything, he reached in his pocket, took out a hundred-dollar bill, gave it to the waitress, and said, "Find out."

The waitress was back within five minutes with the lead blonde's name written down.

He asked me, "Do you think she will go away with me for a couple of weeks to the Mediterranean or maybe Paris?"

I shook my head and thought, *I need to call the fire department to hose him down.*

Mercifully, the show ended, but Mahmoud's son still wanted to go meet her.

Finally, I gave in and suggested that we wait about half an hour or so to let her change and freshen up. What a stroke of genius on my part. When we went backstage to try to meet her, we found out she had just left the casino to go home.

Mahmoud's son said, "Where does she live? We'll go over there right now! I'll get us a cab."

I said, "No. No. No," each *no* becoming a little louder. "You can wait until tomorrow and meet her tomorrow afternoon. I'll set it up."

Suddenly, he thought I was a hero!

I thought, *When Mahmoud finds out, he is going to break my neck or send an assassin over to finish me off.* I couldn't believe what I'd gone through; I was completely drained, but Mahmoud's son and I were now best buddies. He decided to play poker.

I said, "Great."

Mahmoud's son went to the poker room and found a table. As luck would have it, there was a bar adjacent to the poker room with a glass partition between the two. There was virtually no one in the bar, so it was easy for me to get a table overlooking the poker room so I could keep an eye on my charge.

A perky, attractive cocktail waitress came over and asked, "What would you like to drink?"

I said, "A ginger ale."

"Is that it?"

"Yes, I'm already in enough trouble."

She laughed and said she understood.

As I looked around the bar, I realized I was almost alone. There was one other table with an old man hustling a thirty-year-old who looked like a married soccer mom.

When the waitress delivered my ginger ale, I asked,

"Why is it so slow?"

She replied, "I don't know. Normally, there would be twenty-five to fifty people here around midnight."

Since there wasn't anybody else in the bar, expect for the other couple, we continued to make small talk for half an hour or so.

She asked, "Why are you not drinking?"

I explained to her that I was babysitting Mahmoud's son who was playing poker right over there.

She said, "He's a good-looking kid. You've probably got your hands full."

"If you only knew."

I ended up staying in the bar until about 3:00 a.m., when Mahmoud's son got tired of playing cards. By then he had already seen me in the bar watching him, so he came into the bar and told me he was going to bed. I was also tired, and pretty soon I would probably be going to bed myself. I watched him all the way to the elevators and thought I'd wait fifteen minutes to see if he changed his mind.

The waitress came over and said, "You know, he really is handsome. Are you really babysitting him?"

"Yeah, really!"

"Good luck. You're going to need it."

I left, and just before I went to bed I asked for a wakeup

call at 7:30 a.m.

About 8:00 a.m. I had on my walking clothes and left the casino for a walk. I couldn't believe how crisp and fresh the mountain ozone made the air smell. It was really nice. I walked north out of town with Lake Tahoe on my left and the mountains on my right, going past the golf course and the ski lift.

I wasn't really paying attention because I was enjoying the sites and nice weather. Normally, I walk three to four miles. I had already walked almost four miles one way, and I needed to get back. I turned around and headed back. I can tell you that at about six and a half miles my thighs started to tighten. At seven miles my shins began to give me occasional shooting pain. When I got back, I immediately went to the front desk and asked where the men's health club was.

The lady said, "Just keep to your left at the end of this hall."

It was now about ten o'clock. I immediately went into the locker room and asked if they had a sauna.

The guy said, "Sure. Just go by the two swimming pools, and it's on your right."

I immediately stripped down, grabbed a towel, and went into the sauna.

I had no sooner entered the sauna than Mahmoud

said, "Hi. Having a good time?"

I said, "Hi," and sat down. I was whipped. I told Mahmoud that his son and I had had a good time last night, but that he was a handful to control.

He said, "Well, yes, he takes after his dad."

I've had sinus problems for forever, including two previous sinus surgeries. A good sauna usually clears my sinuses for three or four hours. This sauna was unusually hot because some schmuck kept putting ladles of water on the hot rocks. My shins were still burning, I was feeling the lack of sleep, and I was starting to get bleary-eyed. I held out for another fifteen minutes in this really hot sauna before I said I was going to jump into the pool to cool off. By this time, I was really bleary-eyed and weak. I stumbled over to the closest pool and jumped in.

Holy crap! It was an ice bath. One of the guys watching me thought I looked like a Great White as I came jetting out of the water. My heart was racing; I thought I was going to have a coronary on the spot, as I lay by the pool. I don't know how long I lay by the pool; it could have been five or ten minutes. Finally, I weakly got up and was able to get back to the locker and put on my sweaty clothes. Somehow I managed to get back to the room and crash. The phone rang four or five times, but I didn't answer it. I finally got up about two o'clock and started listening to my messages.

Mahmoud's son wanted to know what time he was meeting the love of his life.

Mahmoud's son wanted to know what time he was meeting the love of his life.

Mahmoud's son said he had sent his love some flowers.

Mahmoud's son wanted to know what time he was meeting the love of his life.

Mahmoud's son had sent more flowers.

Mahmoud's son wanted to know what time he was meeting the love of his life.

There were five more calls from Mahmoud's son, but I think you get the picture. I called down to the concierge and asked, "What time does the lead lady from the Playmates of Nevada usually get in?"

He called back about three minutes later to say she was already there.

I called the front desk and asked to be put through to her. "Hello?"

I told her my name, and before I could say anything, she said, "Are you the one sending me all the roses?"

"Huh?"

"Ten dozen!"

By this time, I guess I shouldn't have been surprised by anything Mahmoud's son did.

I explained to her that I was babysitting the nineteen-year-old son of one of my clients, who thought he had fallen in love with her. It was a case of youth and raging hormones.

She laughed and said it wasn't the first time, but it was the first time anyone had sent her ten dozen roses.

I told her I had promised him that I would set up a meeting between them.

She said, "I'd like to meet him, but I'm currently in a relationship with the father of my son."

I said, "Please? I'm in a bind."

She said, "All right. I'll meet you both at twelve thirty, after the show, in the same bar I was in last night."

"Thanks. By the way, what is your real name?" She told me and hung up.

I called Mahmoud's son, who was thrilled. He wanted to make sure we went to her show again before he met her. Of course, I neglected to mention that she had a kid and was in a relationship with the kid's dad.

"I'll try to get tickets," I replied.

I called the concierge and told him I had to have good tickets to the show that night, and there would be an extra hundred dollars in it for him.

He called back about fifteen minutes later and said, "The best I can do is a table center stage, three tables back from the stage."

I said, "That will be fine. Thanks."

I called Mahmoud's son to tell him we had tickets to the show that night. He had already called me twice more to ask if he should wear a suit or a sports coat. Then he called to ask, "Should I wear a dress shirt with a tie or just a casual shirt?"

I told him I didn't give a rat's rear and that I thought it really didn't matter. I then told him I would meet him and his dad for dinner at Friday's Station Steak and Seafood Grill at seven o'clock.

I said, "Please tell your dad."

This babysitting was getting old, but the good news was I had to be in Houston by 1:00 p.m. the next day to sign legal documents on some properties we were selling. If I didn't get there in time, we wouldn't be selling these dogs, and we really wanted to sell them. I called down to the front desk for a 6:30 a.m. wakeup call and went back to bed.

My wakeup call came a little early. I jumped up, showered, dressed casually in slacks and a shirt, and headed to the restaurant to meet Mahmoud and his son.

Mahmoud was already there. He said he had arranged for me to meet the limo driver near the front door at six the next morning to take me to the airport in Reno. He would be there to see me off. His son showed up with a spiffy sport jacket on with a silk handkerchief in the pocket. I almost laughed, but I held it in.

I asked Mahmoud, "How are you doing with the gambling?"

"I'm only down $200,000!"

For Mahmoud, that was pretty good, given how poor a gambler he was. He had previously told me that he had once lost over $7 million in Las Vegas. You can understand why he got such great service.

We had vintage Le Montrachet—the white Burgundy that was Mahmoud's favorite—with dinner. I think the restaurant charged $1,100 a bottle, and we had two. But, given Mahmoud's poor gambling record, everything was comped.

Mahmoud's son talked excessively about the love of his life. Every time he mentioned her, Mahmoud's right eyebrow would tighten and my butt would pucker up. By this time, I figured I might be on thin ice with Mahmoud with his son talking so much about this one lady. The next time he mentioned her, I gave him a slight rap on the shin with my foot under the table, while shaking my head. He got the message and cooled down. We finished up dinner with a very nice crème brûlée. Mahmoud headed to the baccarat table, while Mahmoud's son and I went off to see

Playboy's Playmates of Nevada again.

When we were finally seated three tables back from the stage, Mahmoud's son was upset. He expected to be right in front.

He said, "Why didn't you get a good table?"

Goddammit.

I explained that it was the best we could do on short notice. The venue probably seated eight hundred to a thousand people, and we were probably thirty-five feet from the stage, right in front!

He then asked me, "Why don't you go over to that front table and ask them to trade tables?"

I said no, thinking *This kid has unbelievable gall.*

He then said, "Look, I'll give you $1,000 to do it."

Again, I said *no* and added, "If you don't straighten up and act like an adult, I will cancel the meeting after the show."

That appeared to get his attention. The show started, and again the first ten minutes of the act were unbelievable.

Mahmoud's son was uncontrollable. He clapped, whistled, stomped his feet, and beat the table. I didn't know if it was the alcohol, his age, the difference in culture, his raging hormones, or all of the above. I felt like crawling under the table, but was afraid I'd be stomped to death! The show finally ended, and he immediately wanted to go backstage.

I said, "No, we have a meeting in half an hour in the bar I was in last night."

We got up to go to the bar, and Mahmoud's son stopped off to play the slots for ten minutes—I think he won $500—and then we went to the bar.

It was eerie; we were the only ones there. The same waitress from the night before came over and took our drink orders. Mahmoud's son was drinking a single-malt scotch, and I ordered Wild Turkey on the rocks.

Then the lead blonde came in. She was as good looking with clothes on as she was with most of her clothes off.

I got up, introduced myself, and introduced her to Mahmoud's son.

Mahmoud's started off slow by saying, "You are the most beautiful woman I have ever seen. I want to marry you and want you to have my baby."

The lady gave him a blank stare, reeling from the shock. She had heard lots of lines before, but she wasn't expecting this from this nineteen-year-old.

After composing herself she said, "That's a very kind offer, but I can't accept. I am in a relationship with the father of my two-year-old son."

Mahmoud's son was now in shock and stammered,

"You already have a baby? How could you?"

She said, "It was actually very easy."

I smirked, but Mahmoud's son was still in shock.

The lady then said, "Thank you for the beautiful roses, but I've got to go check on my son." With that, she left.

Mahmoud's son was crushed. "How could she do that to me?" he said.

"What do you mean?"

"Have a baby with someone else. She didn't even wait for me."

"Welcome to the big leagues. You're going to need to prepare yourself for rejection and problems dealing with females."

"That would never have happened in Kuwait."

I reminded him that he was in the US.

With that, he left to go play poker. I could see him from where I was sitting. I ordered another Wild Turkey on the rocks. Since I was the only customer in the bar, the waitress asked for permission to sit down and talk. We talked till about 3:00 a.m., when I said I was going to my room to get some sleep. In the two and a half hours I was in the bar, not another soul had entered.

I went up to the room, packed, and asked for a 5:30 a.m. wakeup call.

I was dressed and checked out by ten minutes to six,

and my limo driver was at the door.

He asked, "Are you ready to go?"

I told him I needed to wait for Mahmoud to say good-bye, and I went over near the restaurant serving breakfast and waited. The next thing I knew, the cocktail waitress from the bar came up to me. I assumed her shift was over and she was going home to bed.

"What are you doing up so early?" she asked.

"I have to get back to Houston to sign some legal papers on some property we want to unload."

"Would you like a steak-and-eggs-breakfast touchdown at my place?"

"Darling, I'd love to have breakfast with you, but I've got a plane to catch."

She mumbled, "Okay," and walked off.

A couple of minutes later she came back and said, "Are you sure you don't want a steak-and-eggs-breakfast touchdown at my place?"

Again I said, "I've got to get back to Houston."

She said, "It would have been fun," and left.

A minute or so later the limo driver came over and asked if I knew what that girl wanted.

I said, "She wanted to go get breakfast at her place."

He laughed and said, "Wrong. Do you know what a steak-and-eggs-breakfast touchdown means?"

"I assumed she wanted breakfast."

"You dumbass, you just passed up a freebie with a hot cocktail waitress."

Boy! Would I have been surprised if I had gone over to her place for breakfast!

About that time Mahmoud showed up. With my fingers crossed, I said, "Thank you for inviting me out to Lake Tahoe."

He said, "Thank you for watching over my son. It appears you've done a good job keeping the women away."

I said, "Assalamu alaikum." (Peace to you.)

He said, "Wa alaikum salaam." (And unto you peace.)

And with that, I left, and the limo driver drove me to Reno for my flight back to Houston. I really hoped that none of the other Arabs ever wanted me to babysit their sons.

11

IRAQ TRIP: OVER AND OUT

FAST-FORWARD FOUR years, and I was sitting in that ancient truck with the Arabic terrorist-poster-boy driver who didn't speak English and didn't seem like he knew how to drive a stick shift. And he was supposed to take me on a tour of Basra! Well, Poster Boy finally got us going, and we went downtown—which was not where I wanted to go. The good news was that most of the people I saw were not visibly armed. Again, I assumed they all carried hidden weapons—or it was like the Old West where you checked your guns at the edge of town.

Arbitrarily, I pointed to the west, and we started to go that way. After a few miles, we came to a slummy area. I motioned for Poster Boy to turn into the parking area of a large two-story tenement building. I got out. Poster Boy just looked at me like I was a crazy American—which I was. Finally, he got out too, and we walked around a little.

Those buildings could have been exact replicas of the buildings I had passed with the boy on the bicycle when I first arrived in Iraq. The buildings had the same look: outside clotheslines and open, green sewage. The only difference was you could see there had been a number of recent repairs. One of the impressive things that I noticed was that all the women and children were smiling and appeared to be happy. Of course, most of the men were still armed to the teeth.

We walked through some vacant single-family residential homes. The construction was similar to what you would find in the poor rural areas of the interior of Mexico: masonry or dirt floors, masonry walls, limited bathroom facilities, and a wood-burning stove in each kitchen. Some areas had overhead electrical lines and some didn't. The living units were small, probably ranging from seven-hundred- to fifteen-hundred square feet.

Poster Boy and I got back into the truck and headed west. As we did, we approached areas with block after block cleared of rubble—wide open sites ready to build on. I had Poster Boy stop at two damaged side-by-side homes that were obviously not occupied. I wanted to look at some additional interior construction.

The houses had few windows. Each had a small cooking area with a fire pit and one bathroom with a commode that emptied the sewage directly outside with minimal treatment, if any. There did not appear to be any electrical wiring in the houses, but overhead electrical lines were available outside to provide power.

The roofs were made of red clay tiles, and the houses had wooden doors with minimal hardware. There was some tile flooring and some dirt floors like the other houses I had looked at. There was no doubt that any type of modern modular home would be a tremendous upgrade from what a lot of these people were used to. We would probably have to offer classes to teach people how to use the appliances and some of the other features, like fans with multiple speeds and blinds.

We got back into the truck and continued for a few miles, seeing very little other than an occasional occupied house and lots of cleared building sites. Then we drove out of town. It was probably six o'clock by then, so I decided it was time to go back to Kuwait instead of going back to the hotel.

That presented another problem. How on earth would I negotiate with Poster Boy (who understood less English than my dog) to take me back to Kuwait? I thought about it for a few minutes and then had Poster Boy stop at an empty lot. We got out and walked a few steps onto the sandy soil. I squatted down and drew a line in the sand.

On one side I wrote Iraq and then Basra.

I looked at Poster Boy, and he nodded. I then spelled out Kuwait on the other side of the line.

Again, Poster Boy nodded. I pointed to myself and then pointed to Basra in the sand.

Poster Boy nodded in agreement.

I then pointed to Poster Boy and me and drew a line in the sand from Basra to Kuwait with an arrow.

Poster Boy shook his head.

I then took out a ten-dinar note—$34; ten times what I'd paid each bus driver for my trip to Basra—and I placed it on the ground on the Kuwait side.

Poster Boy shook his head.

I put down another ten-dinar note.

He still shook his head.

I then put down the three twenty-dollar bills that the previous cab driver had so unceremoniously thrown down on the ground and stomped on. Poster Boy hesitated. Then he nodded, reached down, and took the money.

The ride back to the Iraqi border was amazingly uneventful except when Poster Boy pulled to a stop in front of an old, dilapidated two-story building. There with nothing else around for miles. My butt cheeks tightened up like they were made of concrete. I braced myself for the fight of my life—or for flight.

Poster Boy stopped and got out of the truck. I didn't know if I should run or stay.

Poster Boy entered the building. Four or five very intense minutes passed before he came back out again carrying two bottles of water, one for him and one for me.

He dropped me off at the Iraqi border, and I waved goodbye, my butt cheeks tightening all over again. After my last experience, I dreaded going through Iraqi customs again.

As I went through the door to Iraqi customs, I noticed a beat-up, old bus in the parking area—kind of like the beat up old bus I'd come in on. I groaned and braced myself for another drawn-out round of border-crossing processing, but incredibly, the guy behind the counter stamped my passport and waved to me to go immediately.

I reached in my wallet and tipped him five Kuwaiti dinars. He smiled and pointed toward the bus. Without hesitation, I got on the bus and headed across the border to Kuwait with no problems. I also tipped the driver five Kuwaiti dinars when I was back on Kuwaiti soil.

By that time, it was about 9:30 p.m. I went through Kuwaiti customs, which took about half an hour. When I made it through, I saw no bus around anywhere, but two people were standing in the parking area. A half hour later, a few more people showed up. After another fifteen minutes, a nine-passenger taxi arrived. Everyone else started to get in, but I hesitated. There was no indication of where it was going, and I absolutely did not want to end up back to Iraq.

Then, in perfect English, the driver said, "Did you want to go to Kuwait City?"

"Hell yes!" I replied as I jumped in. For ten Kuwaiti dinars, the driver delivered me to the front door of my hotel.

When I think back about this experience, I really can't understand why Mahmoud didn't want to go to Basra with me. Think in terms of growing up in a country where you are very successful and travel around the world many times, but you never visit the country situated right next door to your home. Mahmoud had already heard from many other people about the many problems I encountered in Iraq, and probably more, and wanted no part of it. He was used to having everything first class when he wanted it. He was not interested in dealing with the poor people in Iraq. It wasn't like Mahmoud was an unknown. When I mentioned his name to the auto rental person, he immediately jumped to attention. Mahmoud knew he didn't want to go to Iraq with good reason.

I kept up contact with Mahmoud until his untimely death from medical issues in 1991.

12

KUWAIT AFTER THE IRAQI INVASION

WHEN SADDAM HUSSEIN invaded Kuwait, I had major concerns for the safety of the Kuwaitis I knew who were still there. In 1991, after the United States kicked Saddam and his troops out of Kuwait, I started to make plans to go to Kuwait to try and help. I made a couple of calls to the State Department and was told that the US was not letting any US civilians into Kuwait who were not directly involved with the US government's efforts to start rebuilding Kuwait.

Eventually, however, the State Department said they would issue me a visa to go. In fact, it was to be the first visa issued to an American not involved directly in reconstruction. I booked and paid for a flight that day to go to Kuwait via London, which would leave in two days' time.

The next day I called the D.C. office to get my visa.

They told me it would be three days by overnight mail, or I could fly to D.C. and pick it up the next day. I told them my flight left the next morning. Although I didn't think too highly of our State Department, the person I was dealing with came up with a practical solution. He suggested that I go to the Kuwaiti embassy in London and pick one up there. I thanked him and said I'd try. I immediately called the Kuwaiti embassy in London. They told me, under the circumstances, they would issue me a visa. I would have to stay in London for one night because I couldn't make it to the Kuwaiti embassy and back to the airport in time to make my connecting flight to Kuwait.

I decided to contact Channel 2—one of the local Houston stations—to see if they would help drum up some aide for Kuwait. They told me to come on down, so I drove over to the station, which was about a half mile from our office. I was shocked when a newscaster and a cameraman came out and started interviewing me. As it turned out, they did not show the interview on TV because they were concerned about public opinion in trying to raise money for a very wealthy country, even though it had problems.

For the past couple of months, I had vacillated back and forth about what to bring based on TV images I had seen of the Kuwaiti devastation. It seemed every day there were more pictures on TV of more damage. It looked like Kuwait had experienced major destruction. Should I bring a number of electrical generators, medical supplies, and food? As it turned out, I decided to go, find out what was needed most, and then air express the items to Kuwait. In hindsight, this was a very good decision.

The next day I flew to London and went directly to the Kuwaiti embassy. I explained what I needed, but the person who needed to sign the visa was out for a couple of hours. I decided to wait. About fifteen minutes later the head of the embassy's visa section came out and apologized for keeping me waiting. As it turned out, he was a member of the Al Sabah family—the ruling family in Kuwait. He was absolutely one of the most gracious and well-spoken people I have ever met. Unfortunately, over the years, I have not been able to recall his name. I spent a very enjoyable forty-five minutes with him at the embassy. He thanked me, and I thanked him and left.

The next day I flew to Kuwait.

A CHANGED COUNTRY

For months after Iraq was kicked out of Kuwait, we would see pictures on the local TV news in Houston showing the damage. When I went to Kuwait, I usually stayed at the Sheraton or the Meridian Hotel. I had seen newsclips showing the bombed-out and burned Meridian Hotel, the summer palace, and many other homes and businesses. I feared the worst and hoped for the best when I went there.

You know, there are a lot of people who say you can't trust the US media because they slant the news to make it more sensational. When I got to Kuwait, I found that to be absolutely, totally true.

Before I left Houston to go to Kuwait, I watched newsclips on two different TV stations showing the burned-out Meridian Hotel from all four sides. One was led to believe that the hotel was a total loss. The first day I was in Kuwait I went over to the Meridian Hotel. The first floor had sustained major fire damage, but it looked like part of the hotel might be open. That night, as I went by the Meridian Hotel, I could see lights in most of the 161 rooms that were occupied, and the restaurant on the top floor was open for business as usual!

As I rode around town, I saw virtually no damage in the Kuwaiti residential areas except at key intersections where the army had modified and fortified some houses for strategic purposes. Many of the downtown shops had been totally looted, including a shoe store that was completely vacant except for a couple of pairs of used army boots that Iraqi soldiers had put back on one of the display cases.

Unbelievably, I saw ATM machines that had not even been touched by the Iraqis, although I did see one machine that they had unsuccessfully tried to pry open. I believe the summer palace sustained major damage, and I saw a few other buildings that had damage. Probably ten thousand cars had been stripped, and to many of the areas the Iraqis had fortified had damage from smart bombs. One neat thing I saw was a number of hand-lettered signs put up by the Kuwaitis in windows, thanking their allies and saying, "God Bless Free Kuwait."

And then there was the area where the air force caught Saddam's troops retreating in a long column of military tanks, trucks, and civilian vehicles. The US bombed the heck out of the front of the column, then the back of the column, and then everything in between. This went on for miles and miles, sometimes five to ten vehicles wide. I was there with Mahmoud about two and a half months after the event. We rode up to a military checkpoint where two Kuwaiti soldiers stopped us and said we couldn't pass.

Mahmoud told them he was Mahmoud Al Adasani, the former undersecretary to the oil minister of Kuwait. Both soldiers immediately came to attention and saluted.

One of them said to be careful because there were a lot of unexploded bombs, ammunition, and weapons lying around everywhere.

The press and military reported that there was limited loss of life and only a thousand or so people had died where the Allied troops caught Saddam's retreating army. I can tell you that, two and a half months after the Kuwaitis had supposedly removed all the bodies and body parts, the stench of death was overwhelming, going on mile after mile after mile. We had to have killed substantially more people than reported in the press.

When I was there you could still pick up live armament off the ground. I saw artillery shells, mortar rounds, rocket-propelled grenades, grenades, land mines, 30-caliber machine-gun rounds, and rifle bullets. When I say you could pick up rounds off the ground, there was truckload after truckload of scattered ammunition everywhere.

I don't know what size bombs the Allied jets dropped, but based on the size of the craters, I would think there were a lot of five-hundred-pound and thousand-pound bombs, maybe even some two-thousand-pound bombs. Some of the craters were so large that when you went over to look at a truck with the tail end sticking out of the crater, you discovered there was another truck in the bottom of the crater. There were thousands upon thousands of trucks of every description and size, not counting passenger cars—mostly Mercedes. Anything to carry the loot back to Iraq was used. Some vehicles were so mangled that you couldn't tell what kind of model the twisted steel had previously been. Disabled tanks were everywhere. In fact, I took a teapot off one of the tanks to give to my wife as a souvenir.

Coming back from viewing this carnage, one couldn't help but feel sad for such a significant loss of life. The people were slaughtered in the open desert.

BURNING OIL FIELDS

I asked Mahmoud Al Adasani to take me to see the burning oil fields. We drove out of town toward the burning oil wells. Before we got there, we passed an oil well that had already been capped, but the area around it looked like a ten-acre shallow lake of black oil and tar— it was really nasty looking. As we got closer to the burning oil wells, the area took on a surreal feeling. The area was lit up as though from sodium vapor streetlights at night. There was an eerie yellow glow with black smoke belching out above the flames at the tops of the oil derricks. As we got closer, I heard tremendous wind noise as the gas and oil came gushing out of the ground under immense pressure, and noticed a rise in temperature.

One thing that was strikingly missing was anyone to block our passage, and there were no warning signs. I guessed that they didn't have an equivalent of the EPA in Kuwait. I presumed, in Kuwait, they didn't have the dumbasses we have in the US who need warnings such as DANGER STAY AWAY. If you couldn't figure out the message from the roaring gas, oil, and fire spewing out of the wells, the heat from the flames, and the billowing smoke, you were a real dumbass.

SIXTEENTH FLIGHTS, NO ELEVATOR

When I went back to Kuwait after Saddam had left, I don't remember the name of the hotel where I stayed, but I do remember that I was staying on the sixteenth floor. One of the two elevators was not working, and it was going to be at least a month to get it repaired. When I checked in there was one working elevator. The next morning the other one broke down and was not operational again for the ten days I was there. Knowing I had to climb down sixteen flights of stairs in the morning, I sure as hell tried to go back to my room only once a day.

As it turned out, three US Army personnel were staying in the adjoining rooms. I happened to talk to one of them the first morning as I was walking down the stairs. He was moaning about having been in Kuwait for two months without a drink.

I asked him what else he hadn't been able to find in Kuwait.

He said, "Peanut butter. None of the American troops can get peanut butter."

I asked, "Is there anything else?"

He said the work gloves they had were crappy, and they needed a couple of pairs of leather gloves.

I said, "I'll see what I can do."

That afternoon, while I was out, I asked Mahmoud, "Where can I find a well-stocked grocery store?"

He told me, and I went there. I found three different brands of peanut butter, but none that I recognized. I picked out two one-kilo (2.2-pound) containers. I found gloves, but I could only find one pair of leather gloves, so I also bought a pair of cloth work gloves. I then went back over to Mahmoud's house and got a bottle of scotch.

It was probably 11:30 p.m. before I got back to the hotel to make my Mt. Everest climb to my room. After I got into my room, I knocked on the adjoining door. There was no answer. I knocked again. Finally, as I was getting ready to knock a third time, the door opened and a sleepy Daren Kroon—I think he was a corporal or sergeant—opened the door. I asked if he wanted to party.

"No, we're all asleep."

"I have scotch."

I kid you not, Daren, Spencer Bass—a private first class, I think—and a guy from the Corp of Engineers from Alaska, whose name I don't remember, were in my room with empty glasses in less than a minute. When I took out the bottle of scotch you could hear the sucking of air. After I had poured four heavy scotches for everyone, we had a toast to the US. This was followed by a couple more toasts. I then brought out the kilo container of peanut butter.

Daren and Spencer were in awe. They couldn't believe that I had been in Kuwait one day and was able to find peanut butter and scotch. I then handed each of them a pair of gloves. They were blown away.

Daren said, "You could become rich just selling peanut butter and scotch to Americans."

I laughed and told him, "I'm not interested, but thanks."

Daren asked, "Is there anything we can do for you?"

"As a matter of fact, there might be." Most telephone lines for international calls were down, and I needed to call Houston. "Would it be possible for me to use a military line to call Houston?"

Daren told me that if I got another kilo of peanut butter, the non-commissioned officer (NCO) in charge of the international calls at the base would probably let me talk overseas for an hour. In fact, I could probably trade it for anything they had on base, including weapons!

Daren said, "Peanut butter is more valuable than gold to most of the American troops."

By this point, we had almost finished off a fifth of scotch, and they had to get up early, so we said our goodnights. But before I went to bed, I took the empty scotch bottle and put it in front of one of the doors at the end of the hall.

If there were a problem with liquor in Kuwait, I wanted no part of it.

PEANUT BUTTER BARTER

I needed to make an important call about a deal I was working on, but it was almost impossible to make overseas calls except on the US military bases. So, as suggested, I took a kilo container of peanut butter to barter for telephone time to call the US. I think the peanut butter cost me four Kuwaiti dinars—about $13.60—at the supermarket Mahmoud had recommended. As I drove over to the main military base, I thought of what I was going to say to try to get onto the military base. I needed a good story.

At the main gate, I was stopped by MPs who asked

why I was there.

"Mahmoud Al Adasani, the undersecretary to the oil minister of Kuwait, has asked me to contact my partner to see if we could help the Kuwait Oil Ministry with a problem they are having in one of the refineries." I told the MP, since we lived in Houston and had contacts with the "Oil Patch," Mahmoud thought we could help solve the problem.

The MP didn't know what to do. Finally, he went and asked the officer in charge at the guard gate. A couple of minutes later the officer came over to talk to me. I showed him my passport and explained the situation. After a complete check of my car and briefcase, he let me enter the army base.

I had directions to get to the area where the phones for international calling were, but I wasn't sure what type of approach to take when I got there. I couldn't just go up and say, "I want to make an international call."

Then I remembered that one of the major baseball card companies had specially overprinted a set of baseball cards with something having to do with the war operation in Kuwait. These cards were in very limited supply and in high demand in the US by baseball card collectors. If I wasn't mistaken, the cards had just been distributed to some of the troops in Kuwait. I thought that was my ticket inside.

I went up to a guard near the phones and asked to speak to the person in charge. A very personable sergeant came out to talk to me.

I told him, "I understand that you have some baseball cards that have been distributed to the troops, and I'm interested in trying to get a box of the cards."

The sergeant said the only person who had a whole box of cards was the lieutenant in charge. I asked if I could speak to him. The sergeant then led me over to the lieutenant. The lieutenant was suspicious of me from the get-go and asked a lot of questions.

I finally said, "I want to buy or trade for a box of the baseball cards."

He said, "I have one box left that I'm supposed to distribute to the troops."

I asked, "Can I see the cards?"

He took me back to his sleeping quarters, and on the shelf he had an unopened box of the baseball cards.

I asked, "What do you need for the box of cards?"

"Two hundred fifty dollars."

"That is more than I want to pay."

He was firm on the price and wouldn't budge.

I then asked, "Would you consider a trade?"

He asked, "What do you have to trade?"

"Peanut butter."

It was like an electric current had just gone through his body. "You have peanut butter?"

I nodded.

"How much do you have?"

"Let's go out to my car, and I'll show you."

We walked out to the car, and I showed him the one-kilo container of peanut butter.

He was impressed but said it would take two kilos of peanut butter to trade for the box.

"I only have the one kilo container of peanut butter."

He said, "No trade."

I started to put the peanut butter back in the car when he said, "I'll trade you half a box for the peanut butter."

I said, "I really want a whole box." I thought about it and asked, "What else do you have to trade?"

He said he didn't have anything.

I said, "You know, I'd like to make a call or two back to the States."

Instantly, his eyes lit up.

Jackpot!

He said, "If you want to make calls back to the States, you can make as many as you want for the peanut butter."

Deal!

For the next two and a half hours, I called everybody

I knew back in the States.

The real reason for including this story was the baseball cards. I could have easily gone back to the grocery store and purchased another kilo of peanut butter to trade for the baseball cards. That year an unopened box of those same baseball cards in Houston was selling for over $15,000, and I passed up trading $26.80 in peanut butter for the baseball cards!

What a businessman.

MEETING THE FAMILY OF AHMED AL BABTAIN

In May of 1991, while in Kuwait, I decided to call on the Al Babtains. Ahmed Al Babtain had died of open-heart surgery a couple of years before. To the best of my knowledge, we had never dealt with any of the other Al Babtain family members directly except Ahmed. When the emir returned to Kuwait after the Iraqis left, he stayed with the Al Babtain's until his palace was ready.

I found the address and went in unannounced. I explained to the receptionist that my partner and I had done major real estate business with Ahmed Al Babtain before his untimely death and that I wanted to introduce myself to the current Al Babtains to see if they were interested in doing more real estate business with me.

After about five minutes I was escorted into a large

office where there were three young Kuwaitis; one was sitting at a desk and two were sitting on a couch. I introduced myself. Sitting behind the desk was Saud Al Babtain, who looked like he was in his mid-thirties. On the couch was Ossuma Al Babtain, an attorney who looked to be in his late twenties or early thirties, and Abdalla Al Babtain, who was probably in his thirties.

I stayed and talked to the younger Al Babtains for a couple of hours. The conversation included discussions on Kuwait's current needs, problems caused by the Iraqi invasion, the general business climate, where the Al Babtains thought the Kuwait government was going to spend the most money over the next few years, my prior dealings with Ahmed, Houston's business climate, and the liberalization of women's rights. I thought Saud Al Babtain was particularly impressive. He had a quick mind and good presence, and he was self-assured, well-spoken, and low-key. That wasn't to say that Ossuma and Abdalla weren't sharp. The Al Babtains invited me back to meet with them a couple of days later.

The next meeting was with the same three people. About twenty minutes into our meeting Saud had to take a telephone call. There was a problem, and he had to cut our business meeting short. Saud said he was flying to Iran in three days to look at their furniture factory and asked me to join him as his guest. I thanked Saud, but I was scheduled to be in London in two days for important business meetings that I could not postpone. I said I would take a rain check.

Although I had never been to Iran, I thought the trip would have been interesting.

AN ATTORNEY WITH CLOUT

On the trip to Kuwait in 1991, I was introduced to Hamid Al Essa, the attorney who drafted the Kuwaiti constitution. He and I instantly got along very well. He was personable, fun-loving, sharp, and a pleasure to be around. He was effervescent and always seemed to be smiling. I was incredibly honored to speak to someone who had drafted the constitution of a country. We talked quite a bit about the process and how Hamid had drafted the constitution.

I had recently met Ken Verheyen, the president of Astro Unsmoke, a California-based company that wanted to help the Kuwaitis with smoke issues arising from the burning oil wells and burned structures from the war. He asked if I could set up a meeting with Hamid Al Essa.

I said I could, and I did.

Hamid asked Ken and I to come over to his home, and we would order takeout for dinner. The evening turned into two and a half hours of serious drinking before a grilled-chicken dinner. At the meeting were Omar, Hamid's sharp son who was an attorney, and two attorneys who also worked for Hamid's law firm, Badayi Fuad and Khaled Al Boshi.

Ken was in Kuwait to try to do business with the Kuwait government on smoke remediation, so he wanted to know if Hamid could help.

Hamid said, "To do large business in Kuwait you need to align yourself with one of the major Kuwaiti trading families." He said he would be happy to speak to one or two families to see if they were interested.

This is what I had previously told Ken, but it was nice that he heard it from Hamid.

Ken thanked Hamid, and we continued to drink.

We discussed various issues facing Kuwait in the rebuilding and the problems with the oil fields. We talked about current affairs and women.

After dinner, we thanked Hamid and left.

I was saddened to hear many years later that Hamid had passed away, but was happy to hear that Omar had taken over as head of the law firm.

13

CONCLUSION

NOW THAT YOU have read the highlights of my experiences dealing with what I think are some of the most powerful and influential people in the Middle East, I would like to draw your attention to America's understanding of Arabs. Based upon my Middle Eastern experiences, I found that a lot of the information in the press to be biased or absolutely untrue, and it shapes what Americans believe.

Realistically, a reporter working for a newspaper or television station covering the Middle East would normally want to move up the food chain over time. To do this, they would need to make their stories more sensational and interesting to get substantially more readers. With additional readership would come more rapid promotions and awards.

The average American has been led to believe by the

media that the real power in the Middle East is within each country's royal families. Based on my experience, I do not believe this to be completely true.

Each of these Middle Eastern countries has thirty to fifty merchant families that have accumulated mind-boggling amounts of wealth by supplying goods and services to various royal family members. In addition, these merchant families have family members who permeate the governments as employees at the highest levels. I'm not saying royal families don't have power; they do have substantial power in their countries. The media just doesn't mention the tremendous power and influence of the merchant families.

Another issue I have with the media concerns reporting about the relationship between Israel and the Arabs. The media typically reports a very adversarial relationship. That may be true among the less educated and less wealthy, but within the wealthy merchant class, the typical comment about their relationship might be, "We don't care whether Israel or the Arabs win; all we want is to maintain our capital and lifestyle."

On more than one occasion I personally saw some of these Arab families give substantial amounts of money, under the table, to support Israeli causes.

The media doesn't mention that behind closed doors,

just about anything is possible.

The people I dealt with were honest, better educated than I was, could correct my English as I spoke, spoke many other languages, gave to many charities, had personal connections at the highest levels, were more worldly and up to date on current affairs than me, had diplomatic passports and in general were a pleasure to be around. This absolutely was not what I saw in the press nor what I expected when I started dealing with the Arabs in the middle east.

In general, I felt safer in Kuwait than I felt walking down a street at night in Houston. From 1981-1986, the murder rate in Kuwait was probably about 1% of the murder rate in Houston. The only times I had major fear for my personal well being were the meetings with the different Mullahs in the desert and during my trip to Iraq.

After Suddam Hussein's troops withdrew from Kuwait, local Houston TV stations showed the Meridian Hotel in Kuwait City as a total loss. This was not true. The first floor appeared to suffer the only major damage.

I don't remember the local press in Houston reporting that a Kuwaiti couple was sentenced to a year in jail for kissing in public. On my first trip to Kuwait, this topic headlined a local paper in Kuwait. It definitely did give me more incentive to obey all the Kuwaiti laws.

I was offered the first visa as an American citizen to go to Kuwait after Saddam left. The US reported a huge amount of visible damage from the war. I saw the burning oil wells. It is true that six- to seven-hundred oil wells were put on fire, and one of the major residences of the Royal Family was destroyed. Major retail establishments were looted. By and large, I saw very little other major damage other than to some strategically located homes and a few commercial buildings. Reports I saw in the US papers were very much exaggerated.

The press also didn't report that most people living in Kuwait were not Kuwaiti citizens. They were predominately immigrant laborers working to get things done.

In summary, here are a number of facts from my experience with Arabs that illustrate the dramatic misconceptions most Americans have:

The people in power that I dealt with were much better educated than I would have ever thought before I started dealing with them. Many were educated at Harvard, Wharton, MIT, London School of Economics, Sorbonne, Oxford, etc.

Most of the people I dealt with could correct my English and spoke many languages.

The people I dealt with were generally open about everything. When I asked a question, they usually did not try to duck the question, but answered to the best of their ability.

The people were more up-to-date on foreign affairs than most Americans.

Most of the Arabs were not adversarial when they spoke about Israel and many gave to Israeli causes under the table.

They were not wild-eyed terrorists.

In general, they did treat their women as second-class citizens although the women in general were well educated.

Only once in business did I run into a woman executive.

Most of the people were extremely well mannered.

Most people did not want to rock the boat. It was an attitude of "live and let live."

I heard very little cursing.

I overheard virtually no threats at any time to anyone whether it was to me, associates or overhearing their speaking to someone else.

Virtually all the men drank alcohol.

Only once did I see or hear anything about drugs.

These people were generally decision makers at the higher levels.

The people I dealt with didn't knowingly misrepresent

anything.

In general, they were not workaholics and they enjoyed their toys—cars, boats, and so on.

I noticed very little art in the houses.

When I was being entertained, there were usually no women or children around.

Did any of those ideas surprise you?

Through those years of bumbling along with the Arabs as business partners and friends, I came to understand that many of my preconceived ideas about them were wrong. What I had learned in America at a younger age about Arabs and the Middle East was absolutely not true. Unfortunately, misconceptions shaped the prevailing thoughts of most of the people I grew up with. I hope that *Bumbling With the Arabs shatters some of those misconceptions with a few laughs along the way.*

ABOUT THE AUTHOR

B EN KOSHKIN GRADUATED from Lamar University in 1967 with a BBA in marketing and economics and received an MBA in finance and industrial relations from the University of Michigan in 1969.

Mr. Koshkin has worked in real estate for over five decades and has brokered over one billion dollars in land sales. He owned and operated one of the most extensive home repair operations in Houston during the late 1980s and started his first land development business fifty-six years ago. Previously, he taught evening real estate courses at Houston Community College, yet his body of work extends far beyond Houston's city limits.

Currently, Mr. Koshkin consults on land development in the Houston area and is involved with numerous service and charitable organizations. He has served on various committees for the Houston Association of Realtors, the City of Houston (Mayor's Committee on Americans with Disabilities Act), and Habitat for Humanity, as well as serving as chairman of Service Organization Benefiting Recovery, director of various Municipal Utility Districts and homeowners' associations, and president of the Houston Executives Breakfast Club.

Mr. Koshkin and his wife, Sheri, still reside in the Houston area. When not working or serving in his areas of expertise, he spends time with his family and long-time friends.

www.ingramcontent.com/pod-product-compliance
Lightning Source LLC
Chambersburg PA
CBHW051522260626
47170CB00003B/750